INTERNATIONAL BEST SELLING AUTHOR

I CAN'T SAY THAT!

COREY GILBERT, PHD, LPC

I Can't Say That!

Praise for "I can't Say That!"

5 Star Review
Must-Read! July 5
A must-read for all parents! I've already passed this book along to a family member and have started implementing what I've learned with my two toddlers. I'm so thankful to have read this book now. I wish my parents would have taken this approach. They literally said "you'll figure it out after you're married." And that was all the sex education I received other than "don't do it..." Thank you for helping me do better for my kids and not being so fearful when it comes to micro-conversations about sex and how God created our bodies.

5 Star Review
Highly recommended for new parents AND not so new parents July 2
This book is thought provoking and inspiring to me. It is on my gift list for new parents now. I appreciate Dr. Gilbert's urgency on this topic to develop a biblical sexual ethic and start "micro-conversations" early in our children's lives on the topics of gender and sexuality. This book will bolster your confidence in parenting through topics that have been historically avoided within parent-child relationships.

5 Star Review
A must read for parents or those who work with kids. Excellent resource. June 29
Sex is everywhere you look in our culture. It is so important for parents and youth workers to be prepared to discuss all of these topics. If we don't talk to our children about God's design for sex and marriage. Who will? This is an excellent book to help you

not only be able to talk to your kids but to also prepare them for what they will see and hear in the world
around them.

5 Star Review
A Must Have Resource for Parents! June 26
I wish this book had been around when I was a kid.
My exposure to "the talk" about sex occurred about 30
minutes before my Dad flew off to Vietnam (1967) a
few months before my 13th birthday. My Dad had written down some notes in a small spiral notebook and
went through them like a military commander giving
his troops a briefing. There was no time for questions
and he took his notebook with him! He was clearly
uncomfortable with the topic and didn't realize I had already been struggling for years with raging hormones
because we didn't talk about such things in our home.
Needless to say, I grew up pretty confused and easily influenced by the world around me. I made a lot of
mistakes. When I became a father I was determined to
not repeat the same mistake my Dad did. I purchased
a number of age-appropriate Christian books and VHS
videos for my children and told them if they had any
questions to talk to me or their Mom. I didn't find out
until much later my children struggled with much the
same issues nor did I appreciate the negative influence modern technology would have in their lives. If
I could have a do over, I most definitely would get Dr.
G's book and engage my children in "micro-conversations" rather than wait until the perfect moment to have
"the talk." The book covers a wide range of topics from
a biblical perspective beginning with parental education and shows how we as parents can lovingly talk
to our children about sex and other issues they are
constantly exposed to such as gender identity, homosexuality, and same-sex attraction. In the world that

we are living in today and our children our growing up in there is no more valuable resource than Dr. G's book to help us navigate these trying times and raising godly, healthy children. I cannot recommend his book highly enough. Great job, Dr. G!

5 Star Review
Complex yet very important topic to address... June 23
I am glad that Dr. Gilbert chose to address this complex yet very important topic in this book. This is a great guide for any parent who is conscious about this topic and what kind of impact it has on their children. This book will get the ball rolling in the right direction. Enjoy!

5 Star Review
Thank you! June 11
Thank you for making the unspeakable speakable! Your insight into how to make this topic manageable while raising healthy children is profound yet simple. Thank you for the encouragement to do this is a way that lasts and the instructions on how to shape our family for the long haul. Truly a great book!

5 Star Review
helpful even if you aren't biblical June 11
I appreciated that Cory took on the tough topic of speaking to your children about hard things. There isn't a playbook for it. This is an excellent guidebook to get you started on the right conversations!

5 Star Review
Equip Yourself! April 12
Lots of helpful information to prepare parents to talk to their kids about sexual issues. I enjoyed the way the author integrated neuroscience and a Biblical world view.

5 Star Review
This is that hidden secret that more people need to talk about, because there is help available! April 8
Dr. Gilbert, I will admit that my eyes were definitely shut and my ears were closed. But as I began to tell family and friends about your book, the more people begin to open up and share stories personally or about their own experiences within their families.

This is truly a book that's written for any person to be able to share with friends families or to know that there is help that is available so that you do not have to fix or Phil that you're absolutely alone and helpless.

It still takes a village to raise a child and we need to get more honest about that reality. Thank you, Dr. Gilbert, for sharing your passion and letting people know what help is available.

5 Star Review
A good read April 8
This book is very accessible. There is a good deal of reference material, but the majority of the book reads equal parts anecdotal and stated factual information. It's a good read that I finished in just under a week.

COREY GILBERT, PHD, LPC

I CAN'T SAY THAT!

GOING BEYOND "THE TALK": EQUIPPING YOUR CHILDREN TO MAKE CHOICES ABOUT SEXUALITY AND GENDER FROM A BIBLICAL SEXUAL ETHIC

I Can't Say That!

Giong Beyond "The Talk": Equipping Your Children to Make Choices About Sexuality and Gender From a Biblical Sexual Ethic

Published by Rebel Press
Austin, TX
www.RebelPress.com

ISBN: 978-1-64339-903-4

Printed in the United States of America

This book is dedicated to parents around the world who want something different for their children and are willing to engage in the difficult work and conversations to change their futures – and in turn change the world. God is faithful!

ACKNOWLEDGEMENTS

I want to thank my children, Alex, Blaize, and Mylie, who are key players in my life, my teaching, and my worldview. I thank God for allowing me to be your dad. It is an honor and privilege –both in the fun times and in difficult conversations.

I want to thank my parents, John and Jane, and Kelly's parents, Ken and Ginger, for being examples to us of parents and leaders that submitted themselves to God's will and plan for their lives. We know this was not always easy. Thank you for the example you set of commitment to each other, your families, the local church, and the Lord.

I want to thank my counseling and coaching clients for their trust in me as we work towards difficult change and growth.

I want to thank my college students over the years that have gone on to change the world through their passions, interests and gifting. I'm so proud of you and how you lead, what you stand for, and how you live out marriage and your family priorities. It is not easy as many of you have seen and experienced.

I want to thank Chandler Bolt from Self-Publishing School. Thank you for getting all this started for me. You are inspiring.

(self-publishingschool.com)

I also want to thank Rob Kosberg and team at Best Sellerg Publisher for your hard work and inspiration.

(bestsellerpublishing.org)

Finally, I must continue to pour out thanks to my wife and best friend, Kelly. You are amazing. I am so thankful for you and your dedication, care, and commitment to me and us. I would not be where I am without your love and support, not to mention your overwhelming care for me during my health crises.

CONTENTS

COREY GILBERT, PHD, LPC

I CAN'T SAY THAT!

INTERNATIONAL BEST SELLER

CHAPTER 1

YOUR STORY: TAKING INVENTORY

Jim and Sara sincerely desired to raise children that love God and make wise decisions. They had done everything they knew to prepare their children for adulthood, independence, managing money, handling conflict, crises of faith, and even marriage in general terms. They never anticipated that their son, at age eighteen, would admit he had been addicted to pornography since he was ten. He had gone to a friend's house and his curiosity led him to type a few keywords on his friend's tablet browser. They were even more hurt to find out their twenty-one-year-old daughter had been molested by a family friend, which led to very promiscuous teen years and a serious sexual identity crisis in college.

Frank and Tammy both came from very difficult homes where abuse of all kinds was the norm. They found each other later in life, married, and soon had three children. They were adamant that their children would never experience the life they had. They protected them at all costs. Their lives revolved around those three bundles of energy and joy. By the time their third child reached adulthood, they were heart broken by the choices they were seeing all their children make.

Where had they gone wrong?

What could they have done differently?

What was missing?

Ted and Jenny are newlyweds with a blended family. They have six kids between them, all under the age of twelve. They have serious doubts about their ability to do this well. They have decided to reach out for help now, before their kids get much older. They know this is going to be tough and that they will face a variety of challenges. They are preparing themselves for what's to come because of what they found in a book like this one and help from a local Christian counselor.

You may be in a similar place to one of these couples.

Are you overwhelmed by the world we live in and the very different world your children will face when they are adults?

Does the bombardment of sexual imagery and rhetoric seem impossible to avoid?

What should you do?

Should you move to a farm off the grid?

Can we protect them from this onslaught?

Should we run and hide?

My goal is to prepare you—the parent—to do this well.

I am concerned for parents that have avoided addressing hard topics with their children.

I am also aware of parents that say they had these talks and prepared their children well, but the evidence on the other end tells a different story. If this is you, you are not alone. You may have had a few intentional talks, but the reality is that most children do not remember them.

Statistics show that most children arrive at adulthood without having had conversations with their parents about sexuality.

The few that did have these conversations do not remember them at all or remember them as being traumatizing. I want you to be empowered to have these hard conversations. I want to see you tackle difficult issues that impact your children's lives and see your children's futures transformed.

The Lord instructs us in Deuteronomy 6:6–7:
"And you must commit yourselves wholeheartedly to these commands that I am giving you today. Repeat them again and again to your children. Talk about them when you are at home and when you are on the road, when you are going to bed and when you are getting up" (NLT).

The commands of God regarding sexuality, marriage, and gender should be included in these constant, continuing conversations—these *micro-conversations.*

My name is Dr. Corey Gilbert, or as my students call me, Dr. G. I've been a Licensed Professional Counselor (LPC) for over eighteen years and a professor of counseling psychology for over thirteen years. I have degrees, licenses, certifications and further education in marriage and family counseling, Christian education, family psychology, sex therapy, and trauma. I completed my sex therapy training at the Institute for Sexual Wholeness[1] and am a Professional Associate of the American Board of Christian Sex Therapists[2]. I am also a Certified Family Trauma Professional (CFTP)[3]. I currently work with college students, couples, families, sexual abuse victims, parents, and church leaders, and I see a common theme among many of my clients: **most feel ill-equipped to address topics surrounding sexuality.**

I wrote this book for you.

I want to see you excel as a parent, changing your children's futures so that they, in the end, live lives that seek to honor God.

I want to see your children make wise decisions, avoid common pitfalls, and be different than those around them in the world.

Where does this all start? I believe it starts with a foundation I will call a biblical sexual ethic, or your ETHOS.

Access more FREE resources, including video trainings and more content at parentbook.healinglives.com

Why Is This Book Different?

I am not going to attempt to address all the possible topics and issues that could arise. That would require volumes that changed by the day, if not minute. My goal is to empower you as the parent to have hard conversations with your kids.

I believe it starts with you, and with your own personal sexual ethic.

I want to help teach and train you on the basics so that you are confident in how you reply to questions, building a foundation based in God's Word. Then

I want to give you tips and tools to have those hard conversations with your children.

You can do this. You MUST do this, or someone else will.

The task here is to help you secure and further dive into your own personal beliefs about sexuality and a sexual ethic. **This is for the parent that wants to have more confidence, skills, and intentionality in how they address hard topics.**

This is for parents that feel afraid, ill-equipped, and may already be facing difficulties with their children.

I know many college students that say their parents tried to have "the talk" with them, but it was too awkward. Many more state that **they never had any conversations with their parents about sex, their sexuality, the opposite sex, attraction, or gender.**

Very few state they had a more than one conversation (or lecture) about sexuality in their growing up years. Whether this is true or not, the reality is that this young adult is now confused, questioning themselves, and experimenting in ways that do harm to themselves and others.

What I want for you is the **confidence and strength to lead your children into a biblical sexual ethic** that will impact their current decisions, future decisions, and their ability to marry well. I want to make the harder conversations easier. I want you to set your children up for an amazing, successful future. I'm not going to do it — you are!

A key to this will be the **Workbook** that accompanies this book - with questions and space to think and plan and prepare.

Why Do You Need This Book?

We were never meant to do this alone. Moms and dads need community around them. This could be family, friends, or the church — ideally, a combination of all three. We are failing miserably when it comes to teaching our children a biblical sexual ethic. I want to walk alongside you and help you develop your own personal ETHOS so that you can then transform the lives of your children and their futures.

The book you hold in your hands is only the beginning of an incredible journey each of you MUST travel as leaders of your families. I am eager to connect with you right where you are—as a mom, dad, or grandparent.

The journey begins with the impact your childhood had on you. **Your story matters — the whole thing. Your ETHOS matters** — and you have one whether you have intentionally thought it through or not. Developing a strong foundation really matters — for you and for your children's futures.

This book begins with a look into basic questions about you, your story, and your ETHOS — your ethics.

- Chapter Two begins by diving into Sex Ed 101 with a look at the church and sex, the theology of sex, and the theology of marriage.

- Chapter Three continues our sex ed plunge with a look at love, sex, neuroscience, and some basic anatomy.

- Chapter Four takes a detour into a general outline of age appropriate conversations for you and your children.

- Chapter Five comes back to our sex ed course, looking at gender, homosexuality, and same-sex attraction.

- Chapter Six goes deeper into some of the hot topics that our children are facing today, as well as tips and strategies for balancing social media and technology.

- Chapter Seven returns to the sex ed course with an overview of raising sexually healthy children.

- Chapter Eight continues a deep dive into sex ed with the theology of singleness and the theology of masturbation.

- Chapter Nine wraps up with your journey into building your own personal ETHOS.

- We conclude with Chapter Ten, which is the most important—it is all about the power and importance of community and your next assignment.

My Promise To You

My promise to you is that this will change your family tree. I know that is a bold statement. **I stand behind the fact that this is a key way to transform your children's future.**

Jim and Sara should have entered into hard conversations with their children early on and built a foundation throughout their children's early years. They did not. They avoided the topic, hoping — like so many of us — that their children could remain "innocent." They find themselves now regretting missing out on prime opportunities to teach and train them early on.

Frank and Tammy have raised adults that do not know how to manage a reality that is drastically different from their sheltered and overbearing home life. Protection is a great idea. **Lack of preparation though becomes potentially lethal for them and their future.** They need both. This does not mean Frank and Tammy do not love their children — they do. They simply need to learn new ways to love them.

Ted and Jenny are on the right track. They are wise to acknowledge that they do not know what they are doing. **None of us do. We are ALL ill-prepared to be parents.** Marriage is rough without kids and adding kids to the mix only complicates things. Ted and Jenny are being intentional, proactive, as they see their deficit and gather resources.

I want to see you prepared for more than just "the talk." This is ineffective and almost useless based on the reports after years of research from my undergraduate and graduate courses.

What I propose is a lifetime of *micro-conversations.* This concept is defined in the next chapter.

I Can't Say That!

CHAPTER 2

STOP THE CHAIN OF IGNORANCE

You Are Not Alone

Last year, a friend of mine and I went on a backpacking trip with our two eleven year old sons. We were heading down from Clear Lake alongside the McKenzie River in the Cascades of Oregon. We arrived and took a shuttle to the top of the trail, about twenty-one miles from our parked car.

We began our journey with laughter, banter, and excitement. After eleven miles along the roaring river with gorgeous waterfalls, deep in the forest, we were exhausted and could not get to water or find any place to set up a tent due to the sharp lava rocks everywhere. We were achy and carrying a lot of weight. What went wrong? We hadn't prepared well enough. What went right? We had great gear that we had built up over years. We even had a water filter. But we were too high to access the river beside us and could not get to water to use our filters. This was a problem. Walking eleven miles in one day was a problem. We called it. We hitchhiked back to the car and drove back to the trailhead, camping that night near our car (let me tell you, that was a great night's sleep!). We went home the next morning.

This is similar to what we do as parents. We dive in with all the gear and expensive things everyone says we need to have to be good parents: a crib and changing table, a stroller and a diaper genie or cloth diapers, a bigger washing machine, and a minivan. We rearrange our whole lives for this child coming to crash at our place. It is full of excitement and joy and fear. In all of our planning though, we can easily forget one detail. This little helpless baby will grow and go through many transformations. Do we give more than a passing thought to what comes next? In my experience, most parents do not see a need for parenting classes, at least not in the beginning. Most good parents quickly realize they have NO IDEA what they are doing. It is sad to me that for many people the only place they can get parent training is when it is court mandated because they are in trouble and forced to go to a state run class on parenting. Some churches offer parenting classes as well, but there aren't many and they are generally not taken by most parents in the church.

"I CAN'T DO THIS"

Titus 2:3–5 says:
> "Similarly, teach the older women to live in a way that honors God. They must not slander others or be heavy drinkers. Instead, they should teach others what is good. These older women must train the younger women to love their husbands and their children, to live wisely and be pure, to work in their homes, to do good, and to be submissive to their husbands. Then they will not bring shame on the word of God" (NLT).

This scripture is the heart of this book. I cannot come into each of your homes and have these hard conversations about sex, sexuality, gender, and pornography. This is best left up to you as the parent — as your family's leader. My desire is to encourage you, challenge you, and empower you to enter into these hard conversations because you love your children.

I hope that you will be willing to be uncomfortable because the results will be immeasurable, even generational. Don't miss out on this blessing. It is okay to be afraid. Allow that fear to propel you into action instead of silencing and crippling you.

Do this in community. Throughout this book you will see the word "Community" coming up over and over and over.

Moms — you may have to address pornography and the "M" word with your sons.

Dads — you may have to explain intercourse to your daughter and prepare them to have their first period.

My hope is that this book will encourage you to face those fears and push through because you can clearly see the desired results — a strong, healthy, vibrant young man or woman that is living from a biblical sexual ethic.

Whether this was your experience or not, my hope and prayer is that you are giving this to your children. Be proactive. Be on the offense rather than the defense. Know that this is your responsibility — to raise up a young man or woman that thrives. I know though that many of us differ in our definition of what "thrives" looks like for our children. Is it a good marriage? Going to college? A great paying job? Just getting them out of the house?

Dr. George Barna,[4] in his research on *Revolutionary Parenting* (2007), surveyed single adults and their parents and found that there is an even greater parental goal than those listed above that indicates a healthy adult life.

Dr. Barna found that parents whose goal was to raise *"Champions for Christ"* saw all the other parts of their adult life to fall into place. I hope that is one of your goals.

I have found that many parents have **"Champions for Christ"** as their goal, but do not know what their role is in this process. One of these key pieces of the puzzle, in my opinion, is teaching and leading our children into their OWN biblical sexual ethic. By that, I mean a reason why they do (or do not do) what they do with their bodies, minds, and eyes regarding their sexuality. This is a huge endeavor, but it does not have to be as daunting as it seems.

"PROTECTION" ALONE EQUALS DISASTER

One of the ways parents often attempt to provide loving guidance and boundaries is to protect their kids from certain things. We love our children. We do not want them to experience pain. We want to be able to control and/or limit exposure to things that may cause pain. In this process though, many families, out of love and care for their children, cripple them in adulthood.

Our society has been very attentive to bullying over the last few years which has worsened due to the internet and social media. Many places have become zero-tolerance zones and are extremely punitive — no questions asked. A few groups though have begun to take a different view on bullying. They find that standing up to bullies actually helps prepare children for adulthood. Facing difficulty strengthens us. The real world — the adult world — also has bullies.

Be wary of simply protecting your children. Our protection needs to extend to preparing them to make wise, informed decisions. Yes, the decisions I would expect a three-year-old to manage will be very different than my expectations for a fourteen-year-old. The reality is that most of our children, with a few exceptions, can handle more responsibility than we give them credit for.

Let us give them the tools to succeed.

Let us help them steward access to things they should not see online.

Let us help them steward their time.

We need to let them fail — so they can learn to succeed. We are called by God as parents to empower them to leave the nest and fly–successfully.

"SILENCE" IS DEADLY

Another reality I see in our culture and families around me is silence. I have been teaching a human sexuality course to undergraduate students for over thirteen years. I have surveyed them every year and the data has been revealing, to say the least. One of the most telling truths I found in the research was that they had the desire to talk about this stuff with their parents, but they did not feel like it was welcome and so they turned to friends, the internet, and porn for their education. This is an indictment on us as parents.

As parents, we MUST provide the initiation into these subjects.

How often?

Over and over and over and over.

Weekly might be good for a season, if not daily.

I call these *micro-conversations.*

Micro-conversations are very brief conversations with your child, initiated by you, based on the need of the moment.

Do we want others teaching them and training them on a sexual ethic that centers around pleasure and self?

Or do you want to be the one that builds and lays this foundation?

Silence is deadly.

It is our responsibility to lead our children toward building their own sexual ethic.

I personally believe that journey begins with us, as parents, knowing what we believe.

Then, we must learn to articulate this ethic to our children when they are young.

The Change Begins With You

Bill and Cara are a happily married Christian couple with three kids. They love their children. They want the best for them. They are very active in their kids' schools. Their children are on multiple athletic teams and thriving in these. They are very active in their church where their kids participate in AWANA,[5] choir and other events. On every visible level they are the ideal couple, raising perfect kids. Each of their three kids has made a profession of faith and been baptized.

Could anything be wrong with this situation? I would want to ask them a few questions that would challenge them to go deeper with their kids before someone else does. Have you discussed the friends at school or on the team that identify as gay, lesbian, or trans? Do they know what the Bible teaches on both sexuality and loving our neighbors?

When was the last time you discussed sex, sexuality, pornography, dating, nudity, marriage, homosexuality, masturbation, sexting, social media, friends with benefits, music, music videos, movies, TV shows, Uncle Bob and his affairs, or Aunt Sherry and her various stages of undress when she visits?

For most parents, these topics tend to be off limits, or they are waiting on their kids to ask questions.

We either protect or we are silent. These are key parts of how God made us, and for many—left up to chance for the making—how our sexuality and gender identity are formed.

YOU ARE THE LEADER

The truth is that **you are ALWAYS LEADING**.

As a parent, you are looked up to for awhile and watched very carefully. You are mimicked and are the only picture in your children's early, formative years of masculinity, femininity, marriage, sexuality, what it means to be a man or woman, and how to treat the opposite sex.

You are always teaching.

My encouragement to you is to be a thoughtful example. Be a parent that has thought deeply about hard issues and can provide your children with thoughtful opinions, advice, ideas, and direction, but, even more importantly, a biblical framework for their life and future as a grown man or woman.

Romans 12:2 commands us,
"Do not conform to the pattern of this world, but be transformed by the renewing of your mind" (NIV).

This is a biblical concept that is verified by science. For some of us this may seem like an oddity. I want to encourage you that you do not need to fear science. All research that has been done well points to God's perfect creation. What you think matters. What you think about matters even more. What you remember matters.

Galatians 2:20 reminds us that you can develop your spirit through choices you make—in your mind—and that are led by the Holy Spirit:
"My old self has been crucified with Christ. It is no longer I who live, but Christ lives in me. So I live in this earthly body by trusting in the Son of God, who loved me and gave himself for me" (NLT).

Where are you leading your daughter in terms of her own sexual identity, choices, and boundaries?
Does she have permission to say "no" or to voice her opinion?
Has she been coached on how to handle a situation where a friend, peer, or adult leader is asserting authority over her and she feels trapped?
How are you leading your son toward manhood? Is he kind and compassionate?
Can he handle confrontation, conflict, and his anger well?
What does it mean to be a man?
Has he placed pornography in the right place long before he opens that door?

You ARE a leader, whether you want the role or not. My hope is you will use this time throughout your reading of this book to do three key things.

One: Unpack your own story—address the pain, the hurts, the blank portions—be intentional to learn from your own mistakes.

Two: Consider your own personal beliefs. How has your story impacted what you believe? Be willing to admit some of your beliefs may be unbiblical and need further examination. Be willing to admit you do not know something and learn more about it.

Three: Search God's Word. Have a defense.
First Peter 3:15 states:
> "… always be ready to give a defense to everyone who asks you a reason for the hope that is in you, with meekness and fear" (NKJV).

Know what you believe. Know God's Word.

WHERE ARE YOU GOING?

My hope is that you will be burdened for the sexual development of your kids.

My goal is that you will see that you hold the key to your kids' hearts.

Where do we start? We could start with a list of questions to ask at each stage of development, or key topics to cover by certain ages. I choose to come at this from a different angle. I believe it all starts with us, as parents, and our ETHOS.

What do you believe?

If you have your own struggles with pornography, affairs, or your sexual identity, then this is the time and place to begin working through that. And as I have mentioned already—this is NOT to be done alone.

Proverbs 14:15 says:
"The simple believe anything, but the prudent give thought to their steps." (NIV).

Be the prudent one. Other translations of this passage word it this way: "Only the simpletons believe everything they're told! The prudent carefully consider their steps" (NLT), or, "is discreet and astute and considers well where he is going" (AMP), or, "The simple believes every word, but the prudent considers well his steps" (NKJV).

Know where you are leading your family. Gain the skills and confidence here.

YOU CAN TEACH AN OLD DOG NEW TRICKS

Commit to living as a life-long learner.

Commit to your own personal growth.

Commit to building your own personal ETHOS.

This is the place from which you will be leading your family. This framework will guide you. This ETHOS will encourage you and challenge you to enter hard conversations when you would rather be doing anything else or would prefer to pass the buck to the school or church.

I want to see your ETHOS guide you into the battle — even into the storms. I want you to be strong.

Recent discoveries in science enable us to worship our creator even more fully as leaders and as parents. One discovery that helps us gain perspective, hope, and perseverance in this endeavor of leading our children toward a biblical sexual ethic is that of *neuroplasticity.*

The concept of neuroplasticity simply means that the brain is adaptable and moldable—we remain teachable. Our brain is always changing and rewiring itself every single moment of every day and night.

A second concept that gives us hope is that of *epigenetics.*

Epigenetics teaches that our thoughts affect our genes and how they are expressed. Genetics do not have to be a doomsday reality. They are turned on and turned off based on our thoughts and the choices we make. This is a hopeful, yet challenging concept.

Neuroscientist and Christian researcher **Dr. Caroline Leaf**[6] highlights in her research that we have free will and choice. These are real, spiritual, and scientific concepts. Check out Deuteronomy 30:19:

> "Today I have given you the choice between life and death, between blessings and curses. Now I call on heaven and earth to witness the choice you make. Oh, that you would choose life, so that you and your descendants might live!" (NLT).

Dr. Caroline Leaf[7] has raised the bar in our awareness of the tremendous power and responsibility we have in our minds. One of her key points that we would do well to remember is that we are not a victim of our biology. Another observation is that you are designed to stand outside yourself and observe your own thinking and change it. Think about that concept. What I am proposing in these pages is that you will need to periodically stop, take inventory, and then re-engage with your children in new and/or different conversations — **micro-conversations** — that will guide them and lead them toward their own personal adoption of a biblical sexual ethic. They must choose it for themselves. They are listening—to you, to their peers, to the media, and to whomever they decide to zero in on—so be a consistent voice of hope, truth, grace, forgiveness, and be a model of a solid biblical sexual ethic.

Where do we start? We are going to begin with a basic lesson on the theology of sex and marriage, and take a peek at some amazing findings in the neuroscientific world that should encourage you as well. We will conclude chapter three with a basic anatomy lesson. Enjoy the process!

The Student Has Become The Teacher!

Fast forward a few months and we check back in with **Bill, Cara** and their kids to find a family that has made a few changes. Everything on the surface seems the same—at least from the outside. What has been transformed are the small *micro-conversations* that are now intentionally interspersed into the culture of the family. It has become normal to discuss sexuality, pornography, and the differences between men and women. An intentional ethic surrounding marriage is more than just modeled—it is openly and honestly discussed.

Bill and Cara are more confident than ever. They have resources. They continue to read and learn and grow. They are also committed to staying ahead of their children and the things their children will see and hear at school. They are open about transgenderism and homosexuality. They have openly and honestly discussed gay marriage with care and sensitivity, allowing their children to ask questions, disagree, debate, and feel. The culture being created in their home is one of safety, security, and grace. Another huge win is the building within their children of an intentional biblical sexual ethic.

Without these micro-conversations, the ideas their children will one day believe is largely left to chance.

LEARNING BASIC HUMAN SEXUALITY

Being intentional in your guidance of your children creates stability. Giving them a guide to the construction of their ETHOS begins with you knowing yours.

Again, where do we start? With the parents. With you! With you learning for yourself—beginning with the basics all the way to the incredibly awkward. You will need a solid grounding in human sexuality based on science and research.

You also need to be grounded in a biblical interpretation of these findings and perspectives. You most likely did not receive this in your home, school or church. That ends now!

Be the change you most likely needed yourself as you grew and matured and took on the world.

LEARN WHAT THE BIBLE SAYS ...
AND DOESN'T SAY

Learn what the Bible does and does not say about hard topics your children face today. An important goal in our discussions will be to answer questions clearly with Scripture when possible, and then be able to say we do not know, or this is my opinion, when Scripture does not seem to have a clear answer. In this book, we will only be able to scratch the surface, but it is a start.

I find 2 Timothy 1:7 to be an encouragement. It reads:
"For God has not given us a spirit of fear and timidity, but of power, love, and self-discipline" (NLT).

First Corinthians 2:16 defines our identity and power clearly.
"For, 'who can know the Lord's thoughts? Who knows enough to teach him?' But we understand these things, for we have the mind of Christ" (NLT).

Really? Us? You? Me?

Yes!

We have the mind of Christ. So, let's dig in and use it!

TEACH INTENTIONALLY

One last reminder as to why this is SO important. In my surveying of hundreds of Christian college students over the past twelve years, I can see that **conversations with parents are what they lacked.**

They want and need to hear from reputable sources. It saddens me how many students I have in my classes that have never had a safe place to talk, ask questions, and even just listen to sexual topics in a safe, non-offensive manner. In my classes, I am careful and clear. I cut straight to it, which weirds out some, but they soon overcome that initial reaction. I ask hard questions. I present clear arguments and frameworks. I also realize that for many of my students, most of their programming is already in place, and to overcome the damage from their families, schools, movies, and pornography will be a steep hill for them to climb. In addition, most have already had experiences with sexual play and experimentation. I remain hopeful for them because I know how God can transform a life, but I am also reaching out to you as a parent to teach intentionally.

I want YOU to be the first one to "go there"—not me, their university professor.

I am honored to be that for many. I hope they will change their family trees by passing that on to others. Many have gone on to teach in their churches and incorporate a lot of what I present in their lives, marriages, and families.

Proverbs 22:6 says,
"Train up a child in the way he should go: and when he is old, he will not depart from it" (NKJV).

This is my call to you as a parent to take up the responsibility that is yours and lead and teach intentionally.

Your kids need it.

Your church needs you.

The schools and society and everyone around you needs this intentionality.

These conversations should be filled with grace, compassion, and care without minimizing the truth.

I hope you are also a leader that wants to put God at the center. Let's learn to do this together, in community.

CHAPTER 3

SEX ED FOR PARENTS

Imagine that your fourteen-year-old son, who has been a challenge over the last few years, comes home from a school outing and informs you that he has a girlfriend. You're concerned because you know you haven't talked with him yet about dating relationships.

Imagine your thirteen-year-old daughter comes to you and asks your opinion about homosexuality and marriage. She wants to know what you would do if a "family member" were to come out. (She is asking because she is questioning her sexuality and afraid of your response).

Picture your eight-year-old son or daughter with their playfulness and carefree view of the world. Imagine that this seems to disappear overnight when they stumble onto a website with naked pictures. That site leads to another site with videos of graphic sexual scenes with their favorite animated characters who now have additional odd sexual body parts and shapes.

After only a five-minute exposure (that you don't know about) your child is showing odd behavior and attitude changes that seem unexplainable. You are finding yourself more and more frustrated with these negative changes you attribute to "just growing up."

Your son or daughter does not want to share with you what they saw due to weird feelings and the shame they felt and continue to feel with each passing day that they are silent.

To make matters worse, they have found themselves drawn back to these sites multiple times, which only intensifies the fear of being found out and compacting the weight of their shame.

What are your thoughts and feelings after reading these true stories? You've probably been there or know someone whom has. You have felt that same shame or fear or had similar questions.

As a parent, you may have a feeling of being utterly out of control as you realize that your ability to protect them was only an illusion. You will probably feel like a failure because you had no idea what your child was facing and you are wondering how you missed this and if it could have been prevented.

Let's start with foundational beliefs. **We need to know why we draw lines and set limits for our kids.** We need to have a framework—a theology—for dating, boundaries, sex, marriage, and the like. We need to have an answer regarding a view of homosexuality that is both biblical and compassionate. We need to be proactive in teaching and drawing boundaries around pornography and its repercussions.

What do I need to know to begin dialogue with my family and children?

A Theology Of Sex

I am sitting in a hammock at a camp deep in the Cascades, listening to a group of eleven to thirteen-year-old boys as they discuss girls, dating, marriage, and attraction. They are joking, laughing, arguing, and throwing things at each other when they feel embarrassed. They are revealing each other's secrets, being funny, then being gross, calling each other names, and revealing who likes whom. These boys are from mostly Christian families and represent the range of schooling options.

The most revealing part is their ETHOS—their individual theologies and beliefs.

Where have each of these beliefs primarily originated and been nourished? Our homes. Our families. Our schools. Our churches. By those people that are in their lives consistently.

The fact is that our theology matters. Your ETHOS matters.

THE IMPORTANCE OF A THEOLOGY OF SEX

The church has historically struggled to balance preserving innocence and preventing ignorance.

A lack of education is not innocence.

Being knowledgeable about how your body is designed to work does not rob you or your children of innocence. It may even preserve it longer. It is easy to find documentaries, TV shows, movies, magazines, and podcasts that talk about sex—the birds and the bees—or focus on hot topics of the day. It is difficult though to find a resource that provides guidance as we sort out our ETHOS. Most adults have never thought long and hard on these topics and could not readily explain what they believe and why they believe it if they were asked by their children to do so.

The protestant evangelical church has not had a thoughtful, biblically sound apologetic on sexuality until recently.

In 2018, **Dr. Nancy Pearcey** released a book entitled *Love Thy Body* (2018)[8]. Dr. Pearcey looks at how the separation of the person—one with moral and legal standings—from the body, which is the physical being, has given rise to a host of troubling problems.

Pearcey argues that it is this separation of the person from the physical realities of the body that has given rise to the arguments for homosexuality, transgenderism, abortion, assisted suicide, euthanasia and other troubling issues. What you believe, and how you teach this to your children, shapes their thinking as they grow and mature.

Prior to 2018, the best resource I had found was **Pope John Paul II's** *Theology of the Body.*[9] This work has been made available to the average reader through the work of **Christopher West**[10]. West highlights the importance of a theology of sex when he explains that:
> "the sexual embrace is the foundation of human life itself. The family — and, in turn, culture — spring from this embrace. In short, as sex goes, so go marriage and the family. As marriage and family go, so goes civilization. Such logic does not bode well for our culture. It is no exaggeration to say that the task of the twentieth century was to rid itself of the Christian sexual ethic ..." (p. 13)[11].

If our culture is to be reclaimed,
> "Christians must first find a way to demonstrate to the

modern world that a biblical sexual ethic is not the cramped, prudish list of prohibitions it is often assumed to be. Rather, it is a liberating, redeeming path that fulfills the most noble aspirations of the human heart" (p. 14)[12]

If these thoughts are accurate—and I believe they are—then the study of sexuality and God's design and purpose for it, is a worthy pursuit.

WORSHIPPING GOD WITH OUR BODIES?

Our current culture is facing an onslaught from the sexually provocative to the sexually explicit. We live in a selfie world that influences what our children do as they seek identity, attention, love, and affection. There is more pressure than ever before to engage in sexual behaviors, and the truth is that engaging in almost any kind of sexual play is a recipe for disaster for our children and teens. There is also a tremendous impact on single adults who believe this pressure affirms or validates their sexual identity and/or prowess.

For many teenagers they become sexual with experiences that they didn't expect and that they didn't want. Pressure from peers or pressure from others leads them into activities which they regret later on. How many teens attempt sexual intercourse because it is the cool thing to do?

How many teenagers ask:

Is it just enough to be in love with a person, or to feel like you love a person, to begin a sexual relationship?

How many teenagers are terrified that their parents will find out what they've done and believe it will be the end of the relationship?

How many believe that they would lose their parents trust?

How many parents would definitely react negatively to this news, but in the end only love their children more?

Why is there a disconnect?

How many of us know that our children are not ready for sexual behaviors, but know that our children believe they are?

What if they are a hopeless romantic?

What if there is harm or damage done from a past relationship and they are now seeking out someone else to fill that void, to gain fulfillment or meaning, to be loved, or just plain and simply, to be touched?

Statistics guesstimate that seventy percent of American teens have had sex.[13]

As parents, what do we do with that information?

Are we unwilling to believe it, or can we face reality? "Not my child," say many — if not most — of us. **The truth is that we need a biblical sexual ethic.** It starts with us as parents. It continues and is taught through the conversations we have with our children. The hope for us is that we gain an understanding of how to have these *micro-conversations* from a foundation after having intentionally built our own personal and strong sexual ethic.

We cannot eliminate sexuality. But how often do we act like it doesn't exist, either in action, in conversation, or by avoiding certain topics in conversation?

We must address sex and sexuality at every age. We must provide context, answer questions, and guide ways of thinking, analyzing and deciding as we help our children develop their own biblical sexual ethic.

Sexuality is as much a part of us as breathing. It is an essential aspect of who we are.

Do you treat your sexuality with a sense of respect and responsibility?

Do you treat your sexuality with disdain today due to your own story?

Do you need a fresh start on this journey in addressing your own history and story that created this attitude toward sex and sexuality?

This is an important question and our actions will answer it.

My call to parents is to secure their own personal ETHOS on sexuality. I want you to learn to have hard conversations. I want you to be able to stay up to date on where your children are, how they are growing and maturing, and have those deeper dive conversations — *micro-conversations* — intentionally teaching them a strong biblical sexual ethic.

How many of you went to dictionaries, encyclopedias or other books on anatomy and turned straight to the topics of sex or sexuality out of curiosity?

Where do kids turn today?

We need to address the places they're going to for answers to their curiosity and questions. What kind of answers are they getting to the questions are shaping them through erroneous information, lies, and usually guided by a sexuality that centers around the self and self-fulfillment first and foremost?

SEXUALITY AND WORSHIP

Parents, what kind of sex education did you receive? Was it a one-time conversation with your parents that was more lecture than dialogue? Were your parents embarrassed? Or was your sexual education left to the school, the back of the bus, or your church? What were your first glimpses of nudity and/or pornography? If we want something different for our children than we had we must be willing to do something different.

If you are expecting to tell your child, "Just don't do it," then you need to know that this approach and abstinence programs do not work. Why? They don't work because a person needs a reason to accept the worldview that says abstinence is the best option. Most children and teens receive the opposite message at home and from the media they consume via movies and music. They see sex as a symbol of true love and as a tool or weapon to be wielded. They need a reason that inspires them to believe that sex has a deeper meaning than "getting lucky." It is worth waiting for. They need a foundational ETHOS that they build on as they add information. For many, there have been zero conversations at home about sex. Some have only been exposed to locker room talk. Others have already been victimized and know more than we think. Research quoted in *The Society for Adolescent Medicine* and *PubMed* concludes that, "Abstinence-only programs threaten fundamental human rights to health, information, and life" (2006).[14] I would like to see our children be the most informed regarding the biological, emotional, and psychological effects of sexual behavior and choose abstinence because they have a biblical sexual ethic based on understanding God's design and because they want His best for their lives.

I often ask my students, "How do we worship God with our bodies? How do we worship Him with our sexuality? Is it even possible?" How would you answer this question? What does worship look like? Do you have any room for the words "sexuality" and "worship" to be in the same sentence? We will continue to unpack this as we move forward.

Chastity is the exercise of sexual purity. It is exercising control of your body. First Thessalonians 4:3–8 states:

"God's will is for you to be holy, so stay away from all sexual sin. Then each of you will control his own body and live in holiness and honor—not in lustful passion like the pagans who do not know God and His ways. Never harm or cheat a fellow believer in this matter by violating his wife, for the Lord avenges all such sins, as we have solemnly warned you before. God has called us to live holy lives, not impure lives. Therefore, anyone who refuses to live by these rules is not disobeying human teaching but is rejecting God, who gives His Holy Spirit to you" (NLT).

We are intended for celibacy outside of marriage and a celebration within marriage.

As we discuss chastity, we must make a distinction between repression and discipline.

What are we supposed to do with our sexual feelings and memories? For much of its history, the Church has fallen on the side of repression—don't talk about it, don't think about it, pretend like it doesn't exist. Sex is bad—a "necessary evil" to bring children into the world—but beyond that, don't do it! At one time, they even went so far as to suggest furniture skirts! These skirts covered the legs of chairs and couches so that men would not lust after their curves. Crazy! There have also been genital cuffs, chastity belts, castration, self-flagellation, burning, dunking oneself in icy water, and even gouging out eyes as a deterrent or punishment for sexual feelings.

In a reaction against repression, the pendulum has swung

to the opposite side of the spectrum and you will find people suggesting that nothing is wrong in love and recommending books or counsel that are at odds with God's word. They advise such things as using pornography as sex education for newlyweds or to spice up a marriage. **Many will defer their children's sexual education to the public schools and follow the secular culture's lead on what is appropriate sexually rather than what God has revealed to us.**

Both extremes are unacceptable.

Titus 2:2–8 says:
"Teach the older men to be temperate, worthy of respect, self-controlled, and sound in faith, in love and in endurance. Likewise, teach the older women to be reverent in the way they live, not to be slanderers or addicted to much wine, but to teach what is good. Then they can urge the younger women to love their husbands and children, to be self-controlled and pure, to be busy at home, to be kind, and to be subject to their husbands, so that no one will malign the word of God. Similarly, encourage the young men to be self-controlled. In everything set them an example by doing what is good. In your teaching show integrity, seriousness, and soundness of speech that cannot be condemned, so that those who oppose you may be ashamed because they have nothing bad to say about us."

Verses 11–12 say, "For the grace of God has appeared that offers salvation to all people. It teaches us to say 'no' to ungodliness and worldly passions, and to live self-controlled, upright, and godly lives in this present age" (NIV).

The way we worship and honor God with our bodies is through the discipline of self-control.

When we say that we will respect and obey the boundaries that God established and are willing to sacrifice a relationship or a behavior, we demonstrate to the world that we honor God.

Ecclesiastes 7:16–8 says:
"Do not be over righteous, neither be over wise—why destroy yourself? Do not be over wicked, and do not be a fool—why die before your time? It is good to grasp the one and not let go of the other. The man who fears God will avoid all extremes" (NIV).

My appeal to you is to have celebration with chastity. What is this? It is feasting with self-control. Desire is part of God's design of who we are and we are meant to enjoy sex with self-control and within boundaries. For too many young men and young women, all desire is dumped into the category of lust, so they believe that it's all bad. We need a strong sexual ethic to help us define these boundaries.

There's a world of difference between "having sex" and "making love." Satan is glorified, not God, when a sexual union is coming out of lies, selfishness, lust, or disobedience. This can be experienced by both single and married people. Satan is the father of these twists. We reveal who or what we worship with our bodies.

Romans 12:1 reminds us to:
"Offer your bodies as a living sacrifice, holy and pleasing to God – this is your true and proper worship" (NIV).

The truth is that our sexuality and our spirituality are intimately tied. God is glorified when His name and word are honored in a relationship. Making love is an expression of desire and commitment within the boundaries the Father has set for us. Marriage is used throughout Scripture as a picture of God's relationship with us—His bride.

First John 4:12b tells us that:
> "If we love one another, God lives in us and His love is made complete in us" (NIV).

Some beautiful scriptures regarding sexual love can be found in the Song of Solomon. Song of Solomon 5:16 reads:
> "His mouth is sweetness itself; he is desirable in every way. Such, O women of Jerusalem, is my lover, my friend" (NLT).

How can we dismiss desire as sin with a verse like this in the Bible? We can't. You were made to desire. You are meant to enjoy the sexual relationship within boundaries. An example of these boundaries is set out in Proverbs 5:15,
> "Drink water from your own well—share your love only with your wife" (NLT).

Throughout Scripture, we see the protective boundary of marriage between a man and a woman as the proper place for a sexual relationship. There are no exceptions or exemptions.

As our culture careens wildly about redefining marriage, gender, and sexual behavior, we would do well to remember the warning in 1 Peter 5:8 to:
> "Stay alert! Watch out for your great enemy, the devil. He prowls around like a roaring lion, looking for someone to devour" (NLT).

Are you paying attention? Are you placing more value on God's Word or popular opinion? What about your children?

YOUR STORY

You matter. Your story matters. Your experiences, hurts, failures, mistakes, and traumas make you who you are as a parent. Each of us leads our family out of our own story. We must be proactive in addressing trauma and letting God redeem this so that we can bless our children with a solid biblical sexual ethic that is not hindered by our hurts.

God invented sex. God loves sex. God did not mess it up—we did. Your first assignment is to be honest with yourself about your own biases toward sex, sexuality, nudity, the male and female body, intercourse, orgasms, body types, gender expressions, etc.

If your reaction to the previous sentence is to hide, go silent, scowl, or pause, then we have some work to do. The truth is that a key part of the foundation of a sexual ethic is our own story. The experiences we had as children, teens and young adults shape us. If your parents rarely talked about these subjects, we are less likely to talk with our children. If our experiences caused us pain, we are likely to overprotect when we should instead prepare our kids. The more severe the trauma is in our story, the more likely we are to err on the side of extreme overprotection and raise children that have no clue and must make ALL the mistakes on their own.

Honest conversations and revealing some of our hurts and failures are critical to building children that have a strong biblical sexual ethic.

WHAT DOES THE BIBLE SAY?

The Bible is NOT silent on sex and sexuality. Let us jump into the deep end on this one and read chapter seven of the Song of Solomon:

> **Young Man**—"How beautiful are your sandaled feet, O queenly maiden. Your rounded thighs are like jewels, the work of a skilled craftsman. Your navel is perfectly

formed like a goblet filled with mixed wine. Between your thighs lies a mound of wheat bordered with lilies. Your breasts are like two fawns, twin fawns of a gazelle. Your neck is as beautiful as an ivory tower. Your eyes are like the sparkling pools in Heshbon by the gate of Bath-rabbim. Your nose is as fine as the tower of Lebanon overlooking Damascus. Your head is as majestic as Mount Carmel, and the sheen of your hair radiates royalty. The king is held captive by its tresses. Oh, how beautiful you are! How pleasing, my love, how full of delights!"

Solomon is undressing his wife. He is enjoying her. He is taking his bride in visually, sensually, and with his WORDS. Now come, in my opinion, the best two verses in the Bible:

"You are slender like a palm tree, and your breasts are like its clusters of fruit. I said, 'I will climb the palm tree and take hold of its fruit.' May your breasts be like grape clusters, and the fragrance of your breath like apples. May your kisses be as exciting as the best wine—"

Wow! What a beautiful picture. This is sexuality expressed. This is enjoyment. This is THE BIBLE. Does this clash with what you have been taught about sex and your own sexuality? Let's keep reading this chapter as she replies to her lover.

Young Woman—"Yes, wine that goes down smoothly for my lover, flowing gently over lips and teeth. I am my lover's, and he claims me as his own."

"Come, my love, let us go out to the fields and spend the night among the wildflowers. Let us get up early and go to the vineyards to see if the grapevines have budded, if the blossoms have opened, and if the pomegranates have bloomed. There I will give you my love. There the mandrakes give off their fragrance, and the finest fruits are at our door, new delights as well as old, which I have saved for you, my lover" (NLT).

These are powerful and beautiful words—not words we would use today to woo someone—but listen to their heart. We are meant to enjoy, to desire, to celebrate, to be captivated by, to revel, and to rest in our sexual selves. This is meant for us all, single or married. We were created with desire, but we were also given the responsibility to steward all things. This includes the powerful force of sexuality. The intertwining of our bodies in sex is a place of pleasure, yet it was specifically given parameters as well. God's design is perfect, as we will see soon, in our chemistry, our neurobiology, our hormones, and in God's design of our bodies and sexuality.

A Theology Of Marriage

Have you thought through your beliefs, or theology of marriage? What about sex within marriage? How was this topic dealt with in your church, community, or school growing up? What about in your home? How did your parents deal with "IT"? The reality is that there are many factors that influenced the development of our ethic on marriage and sex in marriage. Some of the influences that tend to have the most impact are:

- Our personal experiences (good and bad)
- Family history (historical, cultural, tradition)
- Lack of conversation (the problem of silence)
- Biblical precedent (and/or interpretation)

WHAT IS MARRIAGE?

What you believe about marriage is revealed in how you

live out marriage. Everyone has opinions about marriage. Many of us have dreams about what we want our marriage to look like. Where are these born?

Our children see us how we are—how we talk to one another, how much time we spend together, how we spend our money, how we parent, and how we treat others. They see our commitment to our church, friends, those in need, and they hear what we pray for, focus on, gripe about, and rage over. They know our politics. They know our thoughts on marriage equality, abortion, guns, and poverty. They see who we spend our time with as a family—and the diversity of those friends.

If we are not careful, our personal experience growing up in our homes and the surrounding culture will shape our beliefs about marriage more than the Word of God does. What follows are some key points for you to consider as you solidify your theology of marriage and sex in marriage.

God created marriage. He is the triune God, the God of love. He is three in one—the Father, the Son, and the Holy Spirit. In these, He is fully differentiated and fully intimate. The love and pleasure of their union spills over into creation in His design for marriage. Genesis 1:26 says,

> "Let us make man in our image, in our likeness ..." (NIV).

We are created like Him. We were created to reflect His nature through our nature. How do we do this? Leviticus 20:7 says that we are to:
> "Set yourselves apart to be holy, for I am the Lord Your God" (NLT).

What does this look like? We are called to love like Him—because He first loved us. We are called to forgive like Him—because we are forgiven. Is it at all surprising that we are also called to be ONE like Him? I think that one of the most amazing gifts God has given us is the ability to be ONE through marriage. **God uses two key "institutions" to change the world.**

The first, and the one we will focus on, is marriage.
The second is the church.

We are created as sexual creatures to reflect distinctive differences—by design. These differences bring us together through our bodies in a way nothing else can. We are created to come together and experience true intimacy and sexual pleasure in marriage. An important aspect of our sexuality gets lost though if we focus on ourselves, our pleasure, and our personal fulfillment as the end goal of sex. Sex is about more than two adults having a good time together. It is also the means of bringing new life into the world.

SEX IN MARRIAGE IS ...

Our sexuality was created to be fully expressed in intimacy with each other. The design is perfect. We are the ones that mess it all up. Sin destroys. Sin corrupts.

The reality we are now faced with is that sex is one of the most pervasive problems in marriage.

It is also a big deal outside of marriage as it has taken root in the lives of those not married — a place it was never meant to reside. If we step further back, we can see its impact on many lives from abuse, pornography, and the objectification of women that affects the whole of society, degrading and impacting marriages as well.

Many have bought into the lie of the world and try to achieve what God promised through ungodly means. One of the world's biggest mistruths about sex is that it is all about physical pleasure, and that sexual problems are a failure to give and receive pleasure accurately. This stems from a variety of sources:

- For many it is ignorance—a lack of education—on how the body is designed to work.

- Others are unskilled and just need to practice—within marriage with one partner.

- Internal blocks—these can be sexual history, relational anxiety, and upbringing.

What message did you learn about sex and sexuality growing up?
What message was taught by your church?
Have you dealt with the impact of that bad relationship that crossed the lines?
Have you processed the hurt and loss from abuse you endured years ago?

Most marriages are impacted in some way by these things. God invented our sexuality. It is not a mistake. It is perfect by design. It has a purpose. It also has boundaries.

You decide how you will live. If you live for yourself, focused on pleasure, you will be let down in the end. Pleasure as temporary as sex never satisfies our soul. If you choose to live for God, you see that sex within God's boundaries provides protection, pleasure, and a natural means of procreation.

I want you to ponder on the order of these three words regarding sex — specifically as you think about sex in marriage.

We have the benefit today of gifted leaders that have paved the way for conversations about sexuality in ways previous generations did not. Conversations that are God honoring, respectful, careful, and not too graphic.

Clifford and Joyce Penner and **Doug Rosenau**, among many others, have opened the doors to these conversations in the church and in small groups. Many couples that "have sex" have learned how to "make love" and their relationships are thriving.

The focus has been on these three "P" words. As our culture has gotten bolder and louder, those inside the Church have begun to listen to ungodly advice and there has been a de-emphasis on two of these and a heightened glorification and focus on the other. In my estimation, the message of today is that sex is all about your "Pleasure." But is it really? What's missing in this view?

Here is some food for thought on each of the "P's":

Protection:
Your sex life in marriage has an amazing effect on your body, your health, and your life. How? Regular sexual activity, with or without orgasm, improves your physical health. Regular orgasms amplify this effect on your body, decreasing the effects of depression, stress, anxiety, heart disease and other health complications. Your mental health is also seriously improved. Disease is further contained due to a strengthening of your immune system. Sex in marriage is also a protection against temptation outside of your marriage. A regular routine—with some spice at times—with your husband or wife wards off the pull that pornography and potential affairs can have on you at your weakest moments. Use this well. Use with caution. Use with care. Take care of one another as partners in life together.

Pleasure:
You are meant to find pleasure in life—through the food you eat, the things you set out to accomplish, and your body via sex. Sexual pleasure is a beautiful gift. Use it. Enjoy it. Give it. Receive it. Revel in it. Be thankful for God's gift of your spouse. Enjoy! Christians ought to be having the best sex with their marriage partners. Christians should find deep pleasure in this

part of God's design. **This is HOLY!** Pleasure is a beautiful gift from heaven. I hope you can find it in your work, in your day to day lives, but there is something special about God's design in sex. Again—ENJOY!

Procreation:

What if this was God's main idea for sex? Yes, it is about protection. Yes, it is about pleasure. But, what if the design served a grander purpose — that of bringing children into this world? A new life that comes from the bringing together of the egg and the sperm. No other combination can do this. God's design for sex, marriage, and the family depends on this formula. What if this "P" held the highest value? Let me take an even bolder stance—what if every time a male and female came together and had intercourse it was meant to produce a baby? Praise God it doesn't every time! But what if this was the intent? If we elevated this "P" over the other two, would we have a different society? Would teenagers and young adults today make different decisions with their sexual choices if they knew by choosing intercourse they were saying they are ready for the potential result of a baby — if God chose to allow it? How does this sound? Your theology matters. Your beliefs matter. What you teach your children will impact the choices they make as they mature.

DIVORCE AND THE BLENDED FAMILY

Jeff is a serious ten-year-old who is having trouble in school. He feels awkward socially, and is showing signs of a learning disability. He could be diagnosed with ADD according to most of his teachers. He has a learning plan at school. He is anxious. He has become unusually silent lately. Why? He has not told anyone. He doesn't know how, if he should or even if anyone would care. His parents just went through a divorce and he is now back and forth between their homes. His life has been turned upside down. He is still a boy, but he is at risk of viewing pornography, acting our sexually, and experimenting.

The chances are, due to his parents' own troubles, that they have given little thought to *micro-conversations* they should be having with Jeff about sex and sexuality.

Sean and Carrie are now step-siblings. They didn't even know each other a year ago. Sean is twelve and Carrie is thirteen. They are now navigating adolescence together. They are battling hormones, desires, questions, parents, and step-parents. Their world just got a lot more complicated.

Parents, if you are divorced, the micro-conversations I am suggesting here are even more important. The chances are high that your children are exposed to an ethic at their other parent's home that is different than yours. This makes it crucial that you address topics and issues earlier than normal and prepare them well.

If you are a single parent, it will be important to team up with others that can support what you are teaching them. This can be done within faith communities and within your family. Do not try and go it alone.

If you are in a blended family, the same advice applies. Be proactive. Be honest about your own story (more on that later). Engage them earlier rather than later. Be sensitive to the fact that you are not your step-children's biological parent and your role MUST be different. That is perfectly okay. Use that to your advantage in how you engage with them and speak to them, raising the expectations through your intentional *micro-conversations*.

Remember that the rules of parenting for a single parent, divorced parent, or parent in a blended family, MUST be different than the ways and approaches others might suggest or even expect. Parenting is much more complicated. It is more complicated usually because it requires a different play book.

Speaking candidly and plainly, you MUST "go there" earlier than you think you should. Prepare them. Engage them.

Build their ETHOS through intentional, careful, short, thought provoking *micro-conversations* that deepen their resolve to choose intentionally from a biblical sexual ethic.

Love, Sex, And Neuroscience

Fascinating discoveries have been coming out of the fields of neuroscience and interpersonal neurobiology. The more I learn, the more I am in awe of God's perfect design of our bodies and our masculinity and femininity. There are no mistakes.

Why do you do the things you do in the way that you do them? Why do you get stuck? Obsess? Get into ruts you cannot break? Why do we desire or feel certain things? What is love really? How does the mind interplay with the body with regards to our sexuality? What is the impact of pornography? Why is the impact of porn so serious — such a big deal? Why do some choose porn over a live human being?

YOUR BRAIN (AND BODY) ON SEX

Did you know that there is one interesting cure and/or treatment for many of the physical and mental health issues many of us face? In his book *The Brain in Love*, **Dr. Daniel Amen** states that sex is an incredible healing force — a medicine. He says, "making love on a regular basis improved mood, memory, and overall health." He continues to drive home the point with a study that found that regular sexual activity "decreased the risk of heart attack and stroke by fifty percent." He concludes: "Hold the medicine, give me love."[15]

What does sex do to and for our bodies? It strengthens and lengthens our life expectancy. Sex positively impacts and renovates our immune system functioning. Sex can also be associated with more joy, a reduction in physical pain, and improved sexual and reproductive health.[16]

Researchers have correlated sexual activity with a decrease in the two leading causes of death in the United States — heart disease and cancer.[17] This should have you very excited right now and anticipating good times with your marriage partner. I hope so. Let us look at each of these benefits one by one.

When sex and sexuality are in the right place in a person's mind and body, the experience of sex tends to help reduce stress hormones. This also leads to a reduction of anxiety and a decrease in a person's violent tendencies and hostility.

One key finding makes me jump for joy as the science, once again, proves God's design. The research concluded that **the key to this poitive effect of regular sexual activity was found in thoughtful sexual activity with a committed partner.[18]**

> Matthew 19:5–6 describes the design in very simple terms: "And he said, 'This explains why a man leaves his father and mother and is joined to his wife, and the two are united into one.' Since they are no longer two but one, let no one split apart what God has joined together" (NLT).

Marriage is the only context for sexual activity. One man and one woman only. For life.

Phyisical touch that is welcomed and safe increases our **oxytocin**. This is our bonding chemical, and when it is released there is a boost in trust with each safe touch, as well as in anticipation of touch. This also lowers our **cortisol** levels, which impact our body's inflammation properties. **Cortisol** is the stress hormone responsible for chronic stress and its effects. What a beautiful picture! **Sex equals closeness, oneness, less stress, and feeling bonded.** What more could we want? But there is more![19]

Sex within the above boundaries leads to fewer sick days, as well as a boost in our immune system. Orgasms alone are known to be responsible for increasing infection fighting cells by twenty percent. Regular sexual activity also increases the antibody, **immunoglobulin A (IgA)** that helps us fight colds and the flu. Forget the flu shot! I think we have a winner![20]

The impact of regular sexual activity with the same safe partner increases healthy hormone levels, impacts menstrual health, prostate health, our cardiovascular system, cholesterol, bone density, and skin health. Our brain works better. Cancer fighting properties are aided in their fight against disease.[21]

This is still not everything that sex can do for you! Other benefits to think about are: more restful sleep, pain relief, migraine relief, depression treatment, looking younger, improved sense of smell, weight loss, overall fitness, health and longevity, and happiness. These are only a few reasons why we should put our sexuality and sex life in the right place— within a biblical sexual ethic.[22]

LOVE AND NEUROSCIENCE

You might be tempted to skip this section, but if you read over it a few times, you will see it explains so much. **You do not do things by accident.** You do not become pessimistic by happenstance. You do not suddenly become more violent or quiet or reactive or fearful. You are guided by chemical reactions in the brain.

The biggest question for me, as I try to wrap my mind around the complexity of how God made us, is which comes first, our biology or choice?

Where is free will here?

Are we just a sum total of chemical firings?

Do we have much say over these?

Are we only biology?

Where is the soul in this?

Who am I?

Can I truly change?

Is the ability to change limited?

Am I free?

Or can I ever experience true freedom?

Read through these descriptions of the brain and what each part does. This synthesis of Dr. Amen's work, among others, is meant to help you get **a quick snapshot of the complexity of your brain—the most important sex organ in your body!**

Falling in and out of love or lust is controlled by the *limbic system*. Interestingly, *dopamine (DA)* acts like cocaine and lights up the brain, triggering feelings of pleasure, motivation and reward. Whether it is sex, eating, taking risks, or drinking water, the neurochemical dopamine activates your reward circuitry. The "I've got to have it" neurotransmitter—or the craving brain—is *dopamine*. The more *dopamine* is released, the greater the reward. The greater the reward, the more addictive the feeling or experience can be.

Attraction occurs when the brainstem releases *phenylethylamine (PEA)*. This speeds up the flow of information between nerve cells, working like a powerful drug. It's been found that the *prefrontal cortex (PFC)*, which is not fully developed until age twenty-five, is involved in judgment, impulse control, organization, planning, forethought, and learning from mistakes.

Think about the reality that at twenty-five a young person's critical decision making center in their brain is still growing through their teenage and college years. This is valuable information for understanding some of their choices. This should also warn parents that their children still need mentoring and guidance throughout this time as their *prefrontal cortex* is continuing to strengthen and develop.

So, the process of attraction and the role of *dopamine* for a man in the presence of a beautiful woman is that it causes the man's *limbic system*, which include the *amygdala* and other brainstem structures that are in charge of emotion, to fire up at the same time as the *prefrontal cortex* checks out. This leaves his judgment area vacant. No forethought equals potentially erratic, unquestioned and even emotional reactions. Think about how that works and the result. What can be trusted? Is this a setup?

The *anterior cingulate gyrus (ACG)* helps us feel settled, relaxed and flexible. It is the brain's major switching station or gear shifter. Healthy activity levels help us connect, give us cognitive flexibility and make us more cooperative. When there is too much activity, *serotonin* levels lower and we become unable to shift. We get rigid, cognitively inflexible, over focused, anxious, and oppositional.

The **deep limbic system (DLS)** sets the emotional tone. When it is less active we are more positive and have a more hopeful state of mind. When it is heated or overactive, negativity can take over. The **deep limbic system** controls sleep and appetite cycles. It is intimately involved in bonding and being socially connected.

The **basal ganglia (BG)** is involved in integrating feelings, thoughts, and movement. The **basal ganglia** sets the body's idle or anxiety level. When it is overactive, we are anxious, fearful, and full of tension. Our feelings of pleasure and even ecstasy are guided by our **basal ganglia**.

The **temporal lobes (TLs)** are involved in memory and moods. These help with language, hearing, understanding social cues, short-term memory, moving memories into long-term storage, along with the processing of music, tone of voice, and mood stability. When there is trouble in the **temporal lobes**, this can lead to both short and long-term memory problems, reading difficulties, trouble finding the right words in conversations, trouble reading social cues, and sometimes religious or moral preoccupation or perhaps a lack of spiritual sensitivity.

Johnny is a healthy fifteen-year-old male. He sees a beautiful girl and his **dopamine** increases and his **amygdala** revs up, which causes his **prefrontal cortex** to shut down. He really wants to talk with her though. How does he make any good decisions at this point? If his **anterior cingulate gyrus** is running well, he can remain relaxed and flexible. If his **deep limbic system** is less active, he can be more positive about the outcome of his upcoming verbal exchange. If not, pessimism and doubt creep in. If his **basal ganglia** remains calmed, he will not become over anxious or tense. Is that likely? If his **temporal lobes** malfunction, he will be at a loss for words and most likely become unable to respond to social cues.

Do you see how this all can go wrong?

Dopamine draws him in, but each of the other parts of his brain can work against him if they get out of balance. Some hormones and chemicals need more activity than others. The balance of our brain's functionality hinges on many factors. Has Johnny had a brain injury? If so, it will most likely have affected one of these key areas of the brain.

Read any of **Dr. Amen's**[23] books and you will see these clearly explained as having key roles in the specific impact on our mood, behavior, spirit, and sensitivity. We have NOT paid enough attention to this part in the past. If Johnny has a slight spike in activity in the *basal ganglia*, he will become fearful and tense. See how this works? Imagine how complicated this gets for you and I.

I read about an experiment in which a researcher made the following offer to men and to women. The offer was to choose between $15.00 tomorrow or $75.00 in a few days. The person asking the men was a very attractive woman. They found that **men stop thinking about long-term consequences once attraction chemicals kick in** and they overwhelmingly chose the $15.00 over the $75.00.

What do you think the women did with the same offer from an attractive male counterpart?
Attraction had no effect on women's thinking process and they chose to wait for the $75.00.[24] Interesting. Yes, men and women are different.

CHEMICALS AND HORMONES

Speaking of attraction, it is found that fifty percent of the brain is dedicated to vision.[25] The *amygdala*, which controls emotion and motivation, is much more activated in men when viewing sexual material for thirty minutes.

The difference in the brain between love and lust is that **lust is fueled by *testosterone* and love by *vasopressin* and *oxytocin*.**
One is fleeting and unreliable.
The other is deeper, longer lasting, and bonding.

Love lights up the ***caudate*** and ***ventral tegmental*** areas of the brain.

The ***ventral tegmental*** area floods the ***caudate*** with ***dopamine***.

The ***caudate*** then sends signals for more ***dopamine***.

Sexual attraction impacts the ***amygdala*** and ***hypothalamus*** which controls drive.

So, what conclusion can be drawn?

That love feeling may be more of a drive than emotion.

Love decreases brain levels of ***serotonin***, the neurotransmitter responsible for mood and flexibility.

Low ***serotonin*** means you can get stuck on ideas — even become obsessed.

Serotonin levels can be increased by exercise, carbohydrates, and thought distraction.

Men who have healthy activity in their ***prefrontal cortex*** have greater empathy and focus and make better husbands.

If the ***prefrontal cortex*** is overactive we can become obsessive, oppositional, and argumentative. When it is underactive, we can become impulsive, easily distracted, and bored.

Testosterone beefs up the hypothalamus—the area of the brain that is interested in sex—which is two times larger in men. Men with *high testosterone* levels are forty-three percent more likely to get divorced and thirty-eight percent more likely to have extramarital affairs. They are also fifty percent less likely to marry in the first place.[26]

Men with *lower testosterone* are more likely to get married and stay married, since low levels make men more cooperative.

The major chemicals involved in the primary phases of love are the following:

- Attraction—craving for sexual gratification: *testosterone, estrogen, nitric oxide, pheromones*

- Infatuation—intense passionate love: *epinephrine, norepinophrine (NE), dopamine, serotonin, phenylethylamine (PEA)*

- Commitment—connectedness, joy, stability, peace: *oxytocin, vasopressin*

- Detachment—losing a love through breakups or death: deficiencies in *serotonin and endorphins*

One model that I love to tell my students about is what I call **"Cocaine Brain."** I am referring to brain scans that reveal that the centers of the brain that light up when we are infatuated — in love — head over heels — are the same centers in the brain that light up if you were to take the drug cocaine. So, you are literally high when you are in love, or high on love! The takeaway — DO NOT make any major decisions while "high" — "cocaine brained."

What follows is a quick run through of the chemicals (hormones) at work in our bodies from a thirty-thousand-foot view, to lay a foundation for further understanding of the complexities of our bodies, brains, and sexuality. This is a fire hose, but it is worth it!

Testosterone — Testosterone in men appears to make them more self-focused sexually. Lower testosterone in men reduces their sex drive, not necessarily sexual potency, which is the ability to achieve an erection. Testosterone is clinically effective for sex drive only in hypo-testosterone males.

Some women have found that testosterone treatment can move the dial slightly if they are hoping to increase their sexual desire. Women with higher levels of testosterone report less depression, experience more sexual gratification with their husbands, and show strength in forming good, healthy interpersonal relationships.

Masturbation without a partner does not increase testosterone levels, while intercourse with a partner does. Desire and response increase or decrease by complex chemical interactions including peptides, neurotransmitters and hormones—not solely based off testosterone levels.

Estrogen — Estrogen is both excitatory and inhibitory in women. It is solely inhibitory in men. Estrogen is primarily produced in female ovaries, but is also found in both the male and female brains. When combined with a dose of testosterone, estrogen contributes to sexual desire and responsiveness in women. It promotes lubrication and vaginal health while also facilitating the action of serotonin, opioids, prolactin, and oxytocin.

Nitric Oxide — This chemical is released by the genitals when aroused, causing vasodilation, which is increased blood flow to the pelvic area for women — specifically the labia and clitoris—and increased blood flow to the penis for men. Medications known as PDE5 Inhibitors, such as Viagra, Cialis, and Levitra, work by helping stimulate the release of nitric oxide.

Pheromones — These are chemicals that are "scent-signaling." They are secreted by sweat glands primarily in the armpits. These are thought to influence how humans mate, bond, and take care of offspring. There is a direct connection between the olfactory bulb at the top of the nose and the hypothalamus in the brain — also known as the "erection center."

Driver pheromones affect the endocrine systems of others. An example of this is when women living in close proximity to other women find their menstrual cycles syncing up.

Epinephrine and Norephinephrine (NE) — These are produced in the adrenal glands, spinal cord, and brain, causing what we know as the "adrenaline rush." These facilitate both sexual arousal and orgasm. High levels are associated with anxiety, and low levels are associated with depression. Chronic stress, sedentary lifestyle, poor diet, and genetics can lead to low levels. The amino acid tyrosine can raise levels.

Dopamine — This is one of the most important neurotransmitters in relation to our experience of pleasure, reinforcement, reward, movement, attraction, and other processes related to sexual desire, arousal, response, and satisfaction. Dopamine mediates pleasure, increases sex drive, and promotes orgasms. High levels of dopamine though can lead to psychosis. Low levels can lead to depression, Attention Deficit Hyperactivity Disorder (ADHD), excitement and risk seeking behaviors.

Serotonin (5HT) — Serotonin is produced in the midbrain and brain stem. It is involved with mood regulation and emotional flexibility. It inhibits arousal and orgasm in both sexes. It decreases anxiety and aggressiveness. It is symbiotic with estrogen. Serotonin facilitates opioids and progesterone, which also mute sexual excitement. Low levels lead to depression, anxiety, Obsessive Compulsive Disorder (OCD), and what has been coined "new love." High levels are associated with lowered motivation.

Phenylethylamine (PEA) — PEA is the adrenaline-like substance that speeds up the flow of information between nerve cells and is triggered in the process of attraction to help us pay attention to feelings of love. It initiates a flood of chemicals into the brain along with norephinephrine (NE) and dopamine (DA) to create the feelings of euphoria and infatuation when we are attracted. This is also found in chocolate—which may help to explain a lot!

Oxytocin — Oxytocin is a neuropeptide hormone that facilitates attraction and touch sensation. According to Dr. Amen, it is your brain's "love juice." Oxytocin levels increase following touch. Once a touching pattern is established, levels increase in anticipation of touching. It is involved in bonding, both as a cause and an effect. The coolest thing is that it spikes during orgasm—by five hundred percent for men. It plays a role in attraction, trust, touch, sex, orgasm, bonding, labor, parenting, and nursing—to name a few.

Oxytocin also has an amnesiac effect during sex and orgasm that blocks negative memories people have about each other for a period of time. This amnesiac effect also occurs during childbirth. Higher oxytocin levels are associated with increased feelings of trust and a decrease in stress levels.

Vasopressin — Vasopressin is known as an antidiuretic hormone. It prevents water and salt depletion by stimulating thirst and inhibiting urination. It is a key thermoregulator. It limits "overheating" of brain areas involved in sexual activity. It is involved in regulating sexual persistence, assertiveness, dominance, and territorial markings. Men have higher levels. This hormone can make the difference between the stay-at-home family dad and the one-night-stand artist as vasopressin is shown to assist in the regulation of social pair bonding—sexual and social fidelity—in men.[27]

Why These Matter — I fell in love with the word *"yada"* in my training as a sex therapist at the

Institute for Sexual Wholeness[28].

Yada is a primitive root and means to know, to be known, to be or become known, to be revealed. **I love that we were created for that purpose — TO BE KNOWN!** We are known by God and we can be known by and know others.

Yada sex is fully sensuous, fully receiving, fully knowing, fully being known, becoming one in the quiet.

This is beautiful imagery. I personally zero in on the last one — *becoming one in the quiet.* This is sexuality within the context of marriage, within the safety and security of someone that knows you, trusts you, and gives themselves to you and vice versa. What a beautiful picture. **You were meant *TO BE KNOWN!***

Anatomy

I know this seems basic, but it is so important. I have found in my counseling practice and as a professor that too many adults do not understand basic anatomy. We are a sexually explicit culture in our entertainment, yet, overall, we are woefully misinformed and continue to pass on myths and lies as though they were facts. We pride ourselves on not being a prude, yet we refer to a woman's vulva as "down there" or a man's penis as "his thing". We cannot talk about sex in a serious context at all without embarrassment, and most people wouldn't know if something were wrong with their body, their spouse's body, or their child's body since they haven't educated themselves. For example, many adults do not know what a clitoris is, where it is located on the body, or its purpose.

There is a current fad of shaving and shaping the pubic hair that covers the mons pubis (vulva). Is this healthy? Is appearance important?

What about plastic surgery, boob jobs, lifts and tucks, and even labia reconstruction?

Do you remember middle school biology and how the reproductive system works?

Where does the egg meet the sperm?

How does it attach to the wall of the uterus, and what is required for all of this to go just right?

Can you have a conversation with your daughter about her upcoming period and the purpose of menstruation?

Can you help her be prepared and not feel fear?

We need to start with the basics. **Boys and girls are different.** Our bodies are uniquely and perfectly designed. What follows are the basics, followed by a brief description of the coming together of the egg and the sperm. We are not earning our medical degrees. We are learning to lead our families, educate them, and help them ask good questions. We do NOT have to know it all. It's okay to say that you need to look something up. We need to have a foundation though that we can expand upon as they grow.

BOYS

Let us take a peek at the unique design of boys:

Boys have a penis and a scrotum. The testes, also known as testicles, are located inside the scrotum.

Please use these terms.

Avoid using nicknames for private parts.

Model a healthy vocabulary.

This teaches them that their bodies are nothing to be ashamed of and introduces the concept of dignity — that we cover parts of our body out of respect for self and others.

Knowing the correct terms becomes critical when harm has occurred and they need to have the words at their disposal to describe what happened.

Boys need to understand how their penis is made—that it is not wood or bone. It rises and falls due to blood flow, and this is called an erection. There is nothing to be ashamed about here.

Boys need to be taught what is normal for their testes — their sensitivity, and how sperm and testosterone are made in these. Explain to them how sperm is made, stored, and travels out through the vas deferens to the penis and is joined with a white milky substance from the prostate. This is called semen. Arousal by a thought, touch or visual stimulation will lead to an erection. This means your body is working properly.

Boys need to understand that there are differences as well between individual males. Some have parts that are bigger, some smaller, and this makes no difference in the end for their future marriage and sexual relationship. Circumcision is the removal of the foreskin and they will see some penises with and some without in the locker room. Internally, boys have very little to worry about in their bodies as they develop.

Stewardship will be a critical part of conversations you have with them. Learning to manage their attractions, desires, passions, and lusts will be of utmost importance. They always have a choice. An erection does not trigger action. It is more like a suggestion, an automatic reaction, a signal.

Choice is always present.

GIRLS

Girls' bodies are quite complicated. Their sexual system is an open system that requires extensive knowledge and self-care. I find that too many women remain afraid of, or apathetic to, their own bodies, leading to difficulties with the sexual component of marriage.

Girls' external genitalia consists of their vulva (with numerous critical parts) and breasts. Their internal sexual organs include a vagina, uterus, fallopian tubes, and ovaries. It is critical to use the correct terms so that you are empowering her to know her body, what is normal or abnormal for her, and giving her the vocabulary she needs to address problems. The pH balance of the internal organs is a critical part of a woman's sexual anatomy.

Girls must grasp the importance of self-care and the fragility of their sexual parts. They desperately need you to teach them. Too many girls find themselves as young women facing their first period, also known as their menstrual cycle, thinking they are dying. Prepare her. Talk about this. Be sure she understands the process. This is the way her body prepares each month to host a baby, and, if conception does not occur, the lining of the uterus that has built up is expelled in preparation for the next month. Each month her ovary releases one egg, which travels down her fallopian tube. Her understanding of this process and its complexity is a beautiful opportunity to wonder at the intricate design and purposes of God.

The external genitalia include the labias majora and minora, which serve as a cover to the vaginal opening, the clitoris (which is the most sensitive part and made up of the same tissue as the penis in boys), and the hair that acts to protect the pH balance and cleanliness of the vagina. Help your daughter understand this. Help her see its complexity. Prepare her to take care of herself with knowledge and *micro-conversations* that make it a normal part of family conversations.

Your daughter's breast development will be another part of her journey that will include a lot of comparison and potential heartache. Help her be a good steward. Help her understand the purpose for her breasts. Part of her body's preparation for a baby will be preparing the nourishment to feed her baby. The mammary glands behind the nipple and throughout her breasts are part of her intricate design and serve a purpose.

COMING TOGETHER

Another example of the complexity of God's design is the process that begins after an egg is fertilized by a sperm. Immediately, the cells begin multiplying, creating a person. Within weeks, a heartbeat is detectable. It is an amazing experience to see and hear this fast little heartbeat. I will never forget how life changing it was for me to hear my son's heartbeat. Life! What an incredible miracle.

In the beginning, though, the tissues are known as homologous and analogous organs. As the baby forms, and prior to the hormone bath, there is little evidence as to the gender of the baby. Around ten weeks after conception, these tissues begin forming into what we know as the specifically male and female sexual organs. The tissue that becomes the most sensitive part for the male is the glans of the penis. For the girl, this is the clitoris. The labia minora in the girl are the same tissue that forms into the shaft of the penis in the boy.

The scrotum for the boy is the same tissue as the labia majora in the girl.

This is an amazing design — celebrate it!

The coming together of these parts in marriage through sexual intercourse is the process we call sex. This leads to orgasm for the man. This orgasm releases the semen that includes millions of sperm, all with a mission to find the egg and fertilize it. After the sperm swim their way up the fallopian tube and find the egg, they then battle to break into the egg. Once one swimmer makes it in, life begins while the egg continues down the fallopian tube. It then implants on the wall of the uterus and settles in for the next forty weeks. While this is happening, the cells of the new life continue to multiply.

This process is nothing short of a miracle. Teach it to your children. Train them to be in the know.

Make these topics a normal part of the family conversations.

CHAPTER 4

TALKING TO YOUR KIDS

Your twelve-year-old son or daughter informs you that they now have a girlfriend or boyfriend. What do you do? What advice do you give them?

Your son has been caught in the closet with a neighbor girl playing, "Show me yours, and I'll show you mine."

As parents, we must be prepared for these situations. This is a critical part of our job requirement, even though we were never given a manual.

Someone will be their first teacher. Who will it be? And what will be the values and worldview that they share with your child?

For too many families, there is a discrepancy between what the children or teenagers are doing and what the parents think their kids are doing.

One of my goals is to help you bridge that gap. If your children make unwise decisions, I want you to be able to know that you did your best, and they made their own choices.

A mother and her two daughters were talking honestly about sex, or at least that's what their mother thought. She had no idea that her daughters were not telling the whole truth. Her oldest had just lost her virginity to a guy she thought loved her, but now wanted nothing to do with her, and her heart was broken. The sad reality is that this parent had prepared herself for "the talk," but it was now arriving too late. Many parents find themselves in the same shoes, thinking that by having "the talk" they have prepared their kids, but finding out later that their children were already educated and experienced. Their kids had never shared with them what was going on inside their hearts and outside the house.

Parents can lessen the chances of scenarios like these occurring by making *micro-conversations* about sex and sexuality part of the lifestyle of the family.

By having hundreds of these short, intentional conversations, you pave the way for diving deeper into the truth about where they are hurt and their curiosities and questions.

When *micro-conversations* are your family norm, it reduces the stress and awkwardness surrounding these issues.

What follows are thoughts and points for you to consider that are aimed at preparing you to intentionally wade into topics that most parents consider difficult to address. You must do it though! **Many parents will find that I recommend talking to your children at a younger age than you expected or feel comfortable.**

What I have observed over the years though is that most parents arrive at these conversations too late, if they ever get to them at all. When these parents have "the talk" they find that it has little impact on their child's beliefs or behavior as their sexual ethic has already been solidified.

You MUST be ahead of the curve if you want to be influential.

Birth To Age Five

A new parent arrives home with their baby, and regardless of whether it is their first or tenth child, they begin
"raising their child in the way he should go" (Proverbs 22:6, NKJV).

In these first five years, the child is investigating the world and absorbing everything around them. These years are a critical foundation for all that is to come. What happens, and what does not happen, in these years matters. Healthy touch matters. **Vocabulary and ethic building occurs, even if very little language is yet present.**

During this stage of life, children are absorbing the *"energy"* **of the home and environment**. As a counselor and marriage and family therapist, and after years of working with college age students, I have seen how **an ETHOS is developed at a younger age than we probably think or want to believe.**

Even if the mind does not remember trauma, our bodies certainly do. Traumatic events impact our mental health, as well as our physical health for years to come. It is staggering when you realize how much of our mental and physical health crises today are simply symptoms of the abuse, neglect, abandonment, and trauma we experienced and observed in our early years, even before we were school aged.

That *"energy"* we absorb from birth to five matters.

IT IS RARELY TOO EARLY

Most parents do not do anything to prepare their child for the way their body will change, or how they will need to **steward** their sexuality. During the first five years of a child's life, these topics are often avoided, ignored, and suppressed because the parents are **embarrassed**.

This must stop here. By missing these opportunities for *micro-conversations*, we are sending an unintentional, but very specific message — that this stuff is bad. Sex is bad. Our bodies — especially "those" parts — are bad. Desire is bad. This is setting an unfortunate precedent of **silence** from them during their teen years.

What I hear from most parents is **fear**. They think their child is not old enough for these types of *micro-conversations*, but I would ask you to reconsider. There will be a first time to see porn. Someone will have an explicit conversation with them. **Who do you want to be the first person to address these topics with your child? Be ahead of the curve, instead of being the last to know.**

What I hear from college age students — those I have spent over a decade surveying in my Human Sexuality course at a Christian university — is that their parents weren't willing to "go there" or they waited until too late.

Most students wish their parents had been a safe place to go for those hard conversations.

So why didn't these conversations happen?

The students wanted these conversations, but they **expected the parent to act** as an adult and broach the subject themselves, and not put the responsibility on the child or teenager.

Too many parents tell me, "I've told my kids they can come to me if they have questions."

FYI — your child most likely will not come to you with questions along these topics.

So, the prescription is that YOU must talk to them. *Micro-conversations.* You need to have these short, ongoing dialogues that are not a lecture, but a part of your regular routine as your family is going about life. **Make it the norm. When should you start? Now. Today.**

AGE APPROPRIATE DEPTH

I know you're wondering, "but what do I say? I can't go there with my four-year-old. They are way too young. I want to preserve their innocence as long as I can." I would ask you to reconsider the word choice of "innocence". Your children are NOT incurring guilt or losing their innocence by knowing the names of their body parts, how their body is designed, or how the reproductive system works.

Here are some pointers that will make this very doable — even fun. Remember, you are shaping a future dad or mom, husband or wife, lover, leader, and adult — even at age two!

Use every incident possible as a teaching moment. When my daughter was four, she stood up in the bathtub, grabbed herself, and called out, "When am I going to get a penis?" This was a very reasonable question when you consider that she has two older brothers. It was a perfect teachable moment. It only took a few seconds to instruct her regarding gender, the observable differences between boys and girls, and that she was perfect just as she was. All of this took only a few seconds, not minutes.

Another time, this same daughter kept telling us that her bottom hurt, which is normal with little girls. It took my wife and I awhile to realize she was calling the front — her vulva area — her "bottom," since she did not have another word for this part of her body.

This is why the terms we use matter as well. **When we use nicknames for body parts instead of using the appropriate term, we potentially create shame around that part of the body.**

It is not healthy to be an adult and be unable to say the words "penis", "vagina," or "breasts," but many cannot say these words without embarrassment due to how they were brought up.

It is also beneficial to know the **proper terminology** for their body when they must speak to a doctor or if they are ever in a position to have to speak to someone about a traumatic event.

During the formative years of birth to five years old, you can use nudity to foster *micro-conversations*. If your son or daughter walks in on you while you are dressing, or in the shower, do not freak out. Respond carefully and close the door without a big scene. While changing clothes after swimming, do not make a big deal as you share a changing room and they briefly see you naked. Can this go too far? Definitely. Your children seeing you in various stages of undress needs to be coupled with dignity, which is appropriate covering. This is caught and taught. Model this.

Be open and engage in answering odd questions.

Be honest if you do not know the answer to their question, but then look it up and tell them what you found.

Your child is processing their gender and gender roles during this time. Challenge the stereotypes — have your son cook and clean and your daughter learn to turn off the electricity and replace a plug or light switch. Help your daughters gain skills and strength and help your sons grow in sensitivity and gentleness. Do not let them miss the opposite of each of these either.

Help them see the choices and the need society has for men that are strong, yet gentle and women that are tender with incredible strength.

BEING PROACTIVE

Remember that our children's preparation is on us as parents. We must remain vigilant on the front lines for our children's sakes. We need to remain current in our knowledge of what is being portrayed in the media and advocated for in public policy so that we will be prepared to address issues our children will be facing.

The impact will be the greatest if you begin *micro-conversations* in their first few years of life. This is setting the stage for what is normal. Will they still be awkward? Potentially, yes. Do they have to be? No. A lot of this will depend on our own comfort level, confidence, and conviction as we **remind ourselves why we are having these hard conversations.** It is because we want to be **PROACTIVE** in preparing them for what is to come.

When my sons were this age, they often played a motorcross video game. I would watch their eyes as each round started, looking for a change. Before each race began, the screen showed a busty girl, baring her midriff, holding up a sign. I was watching for the day it clicked in their minds that she was interesting. The day I saw their eyes linger we entered new depths of conversations. This is being **PROACTIVE**. You will miss things. This will be addressed later, but know that no one is the perfect parent. Even when we are being intentional, we will not be able to catch everything. Grace for ourselves and our children is critical. Forgiveness must reign in our families. We must model these traits for their sake and ours.

Another critical reason we must be **PROACTIVE** is that it is our responsibility to protect them. Abuse happens. Bad things happen. Prepare them so that they will know what to do. If this has been discussed prior to a potentially harmful situation, they are more likely to default to a fight or flight response, rather than freezing.

Preparing them for "stranger danger" covers about **9%** of the abuse that occurs, leaving them vulnerable to the other **91%**.[29] Unfortunately, harm will most likely come from a trusted family member, friend, or confidant that you would never suspect. Prepare them to yell "NO," kick, bite, and scream. Help them, via the tool of *micro-conversations*, to know what is appropriate behavior and what crosses the lines. Rehearse scenarios.

When our kids were younger, we had a lot of babysitters from the local Christian college that I worked at. After we returned home from a date night, we regularly asked them what they had done while the sitter was there — whether they had bathed them, changed their clothes, etc. We knew that the kids most likely would not tell us if something had happened, but we were looking for a change in how they answered — a subtle shift. How would we know though? We would recognize this subtle shift because we knew what was a normal response and the kids thought it was normal to be asked these questions.

As I alluded to earlier, it is troubling to me when I have someone tell me that they don't want to have these *micro-conversations* because they want to "preserve their child's innocence." What does this even mean?

This suggests to me that the parent subconsciously — or consciously — believes that the sexual part of their bodies is dirty or bad, and that to understand how their body works and how to protect it is a sinful practice.

It would be a great exercise for us all to look at our own beliefs about sexuality and determine why it is that we delay having these *micro-conversations.* We have many things that we may choose to use as a measure of our children's success — education, income, athletic achievements, etc.

I want to urge you to consider that an understanding of sexuality and making wise choices from a biblical sexual ethic will set your child up for success and influence generations. The seed of this success begins early — before they are school age — when they are absorbing the **energy** and values of the home and world they live in.

Kinder To Elementary Age (6~10)

That bundle of joy and energy that joined your family over six years ago is not the same person he or she once was back then. Their needs are different; their questions are longer and more detailed.

During this age range, our children are absorbing the **culture** of the home, as well as the world around them.

They begin to absorb the **energy** of a home at birth, but somewhere around age six it becomes more about the **culture**.

Their vocabulary is growing by leaps and bounds. Their opinions an personalities are not only being formed, but already becoming more solidified.

Therefore, **we must stay ahead of the curve regarding *micro-conversations* on sex, sexuality, gender and various other issues they will soon face.**

Imagine your eight-year-old today. He is full of life and energy and his personality is being established. He is changing almost daily as his body prepares for puberty and his mind begins to shift its focus onto attractions and desires.

The average age a child in America views pornography is nine.

Most of the parents I talk to believe and say that their child is the exception. I then talk to their children in college and those parents were wrong. Their children were the norm — hiding behind shame, afraid of being exposed, living in fear, and living full of desire gone mad (lust).

Is your son prepared to face his first exposure to a naked picture on a screen? What about a video?

Is your daughter ready to see those images as she processes where she is at in comparison? This can be a terrifying time.

Who are they going to talk to about these experiences? Do not wait for them to approach you with their questions or to confess to what they have been exposed to.

You MUST be the one to initiate dialogue, asking questions of your own. Keep the conversations short though so you can have them often — *micro-conversations.*

CONVERSATIONS BEGIN WITH YOU—THE PARENT

Most parents would love to ignore, delete, deny the existence of, and never address these issues with their sons and daughters. Honestly, most well intentioned parents ignore the fact that their sons could get a girl pregnant at a young age or that their daughters could conceive at a very young age as well.

This is why we MUST prepare them. It is our responsibility and duty to them and those they have relationships with.

Between the ages of six and ten, most kids are looking for answers — and they are ready for those to be blunt and explicit. Give it to them. Be honest. Be casual, but remember that in every response you are helping them form their belief system about sex, sexuality, gender, and their bodies.

Your silence preaches. Also, the world is speaking loud and clear through movies, music, online videos and social media about its beliefs on these things.

Be a constant in your child's life. There are key areas that ought to be covered during this formative stage when most parents would prefer to ignore the fact they are soon to be young men and women.

You should **continue using the correct terms.** Call a penis a penis. Call the vagina and vulva just that. It is very important that a discussion about masturbation occurs during this time of life. Are they ready? Prepare them for what they are about to feel, desire, and potentially obsess about if they are not careful. Check out some further talking points on the "M" word in chapter eight.

This is the time in your child's life that conversations need to deepen.

Focus on a more thorough understanding of anatomy — as well as what is about to change in their bodies and those of the opposite gender.

Prepare them to face the onslaught of sexual images they will notice at the check-out stands, in entertainment, and people they pass on the street. Be sure not to shame covered body parts. It is about dignity and modesty. These are not "dirty" words.

Take the time now to **establish a foundation regarding dating.** What are the guidelines and expectations of boyfriend/ girlfriend relationships? Explain your ETHOS when they are still willing to listen to you and pray that they will take it in and adopt it as their own — for their success, health and future well-being.

Teach them about abuse more thoroughly — explain the real world. Help them see that there is evil in the world and that not everyone has their best interest at heart. Let them know that they have the right and power to choose, to say "NO," and to stand up for themselves. Prepare them to fight back.

Another issue facing children between the ages of six and ten is **learning to overcome disappointment and rejection.** It is much better for them to face small hurts now and learn coping skills than to protect them from consequences and render them incapable of facing bigger hurts later in life.

One of the biggest questions and areas of concern for many in this stage of life has now become that of **sexual identity.**

Who am I attracted to? What do I do with these feelings? Is this right? Good? Okay? Biblical? Will I ever be loved or accepted or find that one person?

I know that it seems like it is too soon. It is not though when you consider the culture and time we live in.

You want this ETHOS in their heart before they are making decisions with their body.

You want them to have an ETHOS that is so settled and strong that when they are faced with a choice to make, it is a no-brainer for them.

THERE IS NO SUCH THING AS "THE TALK"

This is the age when many parents decide to have "the talk" — a one-time lecture that tells their kids about the birds and the bees and answers all their questions in one fell swoop.

As I have mentioned before, parents report that they have had this conversation with their children, but their children say, "My parents never talked to me about sex."

Obviously, there is a disconnect here. One awkward evening is not going to open up the doors of conversation.

My recommendation is to begin at birth and have constant, continual *micro-conversations* so that your kids can say, "My parents were always talking to me about sex."

Discuss marriage on an ongoing basis. Use stories that you've heard, scenes in movies or TV shows, and occurrences around your own home to teach, train, and prepare your children to have a biblical sexual ethic.

Between the ages of six and ten, our children are on a fact-finding mission about their world.

Boundaries become even more important. What is occurring in your child's life during this age?

I can almost assure you that they have been exposed to pornography. They begin noticing gender differences, their bodies, others' bodies, and their own desires. They are being told by culture and well-meaning friends and family that they are expected to have a boyfriend or girlfriend. **This should be reframed quickly.** How?

Set the stage at home by discussing dating, the opposite sex, and attraction ahead of time — before they are even interested.

Plant the seeds of understanding that other families and friends will expect a young boy or girl to date by thirteen or fourteen, but we want something different for you — something better — and this is why. Teach them early.

CRUCIAL TALKING POINTS

Have you ever intentionally discussed with your son how he should talk about women? Their clothing, their bodies, their beauty, their sexuality, their minds, their hearts, their souls?

Do your sons have a biblical sexual ethic and boundaries?

What are they picking up from you in the way you treat your wife, your mother, and other women around you?

When was the last time you purposefully discussed what men are like with your daughter? The fragility of the male ego, their insecurities, their lusts and desires, boundaries, bodies, differences, sexuality, minds, hearts, and souls?

What are they learning at home about the roles of men and women?

Remember, if we don't have these *micro-conversations*, someone else will. The *micro-conversations* that you have with your sons and daughters between the ages of six and ten are probably **the most critical training** for all that is to come.

Help them to develop a biblical sexual ethic early surrounding their bodies, desire, sex, dating, marriage, pornography and the like.

Here are some critical talking points for you to use to begin. This is not exhaustive, but it is a start in the right direction. Some children are less mature and need less, but most are smarter than we realize and we have minimized their intelligence for our own comfort.

Every child at this age is watching and absorbing our homes **energy** and **culture**. This forms the foundation for all that is to come in their future desires, compulsions, and obsessions.

Will your child remember all these discussions that you have with them? No, they won't. **But the seeds you have planted will be quietly growing and at work subconsciously.**

This is the laying of the foundation.

These *micro-conversations* are giving them places to hang future learning, context for decision making, and the empowerment to use wisdom and discernment to make great decisions when they are young.

In the face of harm, they are much more likely to fight or flee, rather than freeze. This is a huge game changer for their future as well.

TOPICS TO COVER:

Boyfriend / Girlfriend — Be intentional about developing a frame work of thinking about dating and relationships that they can own as they mature.

What is the purpose of dating?

What does boyfriend / girlfriend mean?

What is attraction, desire, and lust?

How do I manage these weird feelings?

Prepare them to say "NO."

Prepare them to question a culture that deems them broken or same-sex attracted if they do not lose their virginity in their teens.

Arm them with a defense that they can own as they mature.

As they grow, what they once repeated because they knew it was the "right" answer, can become their own deep seated conviction.

Prepare your child to see dating as a fun activity that is done in groups, and that there is NO NEED for singling out one individual to date until they have a job, and their own money and car. Parents should not be funding their children's dating life.

They also do not need to date until they are mature enough to be responsible for someone else's heart and the baby that could potentially be on the way when they begin dating young.

Inspire them with a desire for a marriage that will go the distance — a marriage that is filled with laughter and joy and is prepared to endure during the hard times.

Be an example of the kind of marriage you want for your children.

When I was seven years old, my family was living in Costa Rica attending language school. My mother went into emergency surgery and came out of surgery with a mastectomy. The doctors had discovered cancer and it was war — for her life. I watched my father love my mother through radiation and chemotherapy. Watching him serve her through this was a tremendous example to me of what love should be. Ten years later, when they went down the same road with a cancer battle, his commitment and service continued to solidify the type of husband that I wanted to be and this helped me to clarify what was truly important in a future wife.

More Descriptive Anatomy Lesson — This is the time that you need to be sure your child has a good grasp of basic anatomy.

They need to understand the human reproductive system so that they know the effect of bringing a penis and vagina together.

They need to know the "why's" and "why nots" of sexual activities before their hormones are raging and their decision making becomes further impaired.

Help them see beauty in their own bodies and the bodies of the opposite sex.

Help them become protectors and leaders of a healthy sexual ethic. As they live amongst peers that have a very different sexual ethic, my hope is that our children would treat others respectfully and show themselves to be people of honor. This is a huge win!

Teach your daughters — and sons — about menstruation. Your daughter especially needs to know what to expect and what products are available to her. Your sons need to know that this is NOT something to tease a girl about and how to react when a young female peer has a clothing issue during their period.

Help them know how to process visual stimulation that is arousing by normalizing it. Explain to them that their thoughts and feelings should NEVER be their guide — this is usually unreliable data.

By having these *micro-conversations* all along the way, you will have given them a compass to orient themselves when they are pulled in different directions.

A key factor is NOT to put too much emphasis on what your children say, since they will often tell us what we want to hear. However, we want to capture their hearts and attempt to know what is going on in their heart and mind as that is what will ultimately guide behavior and the choices they make.

The "M" Word — This is a real issue. My first word of advice is NOT to be a parent that fuels shame.

Be a redemptive voice. Almost all boys — and even many girls — will engage in this behavior.

Be ahead of the curve and prepared by talking about it. It is okay to express your feelings and opinions, but be careful to refrain from pure judgment. This subject is covered in greater detail in chapter eight.

Boundaries — At this age, help your children to set boundaries. The family system invites this continual activity. Conflicts between siblings and parents require the implementation of boundaries. However, we as parents often do not model appropriate boundaries. For some of us, we deem setting a boundary as unloving, when it is quite the opposite. When this activity is simply operating in the background of our minds — like an operating system — it is less helpful.

The goal is to bring this out into the open via dialogue. Express where appropriate boundaries are with different individuals. You will most likely see improvements in your own boundaries at home and elsewhere. Discuss options and make decisions about what to do when boundaries are crossed.

Move the unconscious reactions to the forefront of their thoughts. It is amazing how this process can change everything in our decision-making routines.

Boundaries are a matter of self-care and an aid to prevent abuse. Boundaries matter in all relationships: family, friends, dating, courting, marriage, and even business.

Pornography — I know it seems too early, **but it is not.** When my middle son was seven years old, I took him with me to a presentation I did for a Young Life group of teen boys. The topic was porn. It was an incredible two hours full of honest and vulnerable discussion, which is not normal. It was a refreshing evening. As my son and I drove home, I asked him, "So, any questions about what we discussed?" His reply was, "I had NO IDEA what you guys were talking about." I probed some more, since it is my job to be proactive, and saw that he was in a good place.

At the age of 10 he often attends classes I teach on the subject. We discuss pornography at the dinner table and it comes up almost every day in some form or fashion. It is a normal point of conversation.

We want to have talked about this so much that they have an almost automatic reaction when the door to porn opens so that they are able to close it. Expose it. Talk about it.

Help your son and daughter see for themselves why this is damaging to their future selves. You cannot protect them for long. You can try things like filters and avoiding all screens, but this only protects them if they are at home on your monitored devices and networks.

What will happen when a friend or cousin visits from school or church and has their own device? What about when they attend a sport or band camp — or church camp — and that door is swung wide open. **The goal is that they know how to process the feelings and curiosity when temptation comes and can quickly respond with a "no thanks," and turn away from the screen.**

Pornography works. It sucks us in because we are naturally and healthily drawn to nudity and beauty. **Create an ethic and ETHOS that is redemptive and not punitive.**

Remind yourself and teach your child that each person in those videos and pictures has a story. They are real people, and most of them are being exploited and abused. For many of the "porn stars," this is a step up from the rough life they were brought up in, and they hope it will be a means of escape. This ought to be heartbreaking. Express this to your children. Discuss human trafficking. Maybe even get involved in some way as a family in helping prevent and/or support efforts of organizations aimed at eradicating this gross exploitation of fellow humans from all walks of life.

Remember that the door to pornography, once opened, can rarely be shut permanently. I've often wondered why God chooses NOT to remove this temptation ten or twenty years down the road and have come to believe that it serves as a reminder of our humanity and need for a Savior. **We cannot do this alone.**

If your son or daughter has opened this door — and the average age is between six and ten — be a listening ear and a place of love, compassion, hope, and care. DO NOT punish or shame them for their behavior. Please do not do that. The voice of the enemy is already at work in your child's heart telling them that they are dirty, broken, irredeemable—that no one will be able to look past this. That will need to be addressed separately. Prepare them for the REAL world they will face today and in ten years so that they can leave your protective nest and soar.

Sexual Identity — Many children between the ages of six and ten are beginning to question their gender identity because they hear what others are saying about them and they believe what they hear. We must be attentive as these questions tend to be internally processed and traumatic.

You can help them by painting a realistic picture of masculinity and femininity that does not tie activities to gender. Help them see that they are their biological sex, and this isn't tied to the activities they enjoy or personality traits. The longer they linger on questions of identify the more they will question everything. I personally know the battle of this one. I was an awkward preteen boy that loved pink and crocheting with my grandmother. I valued time with people and preferred long deep conversations to watching sports. I still do. I loved music and played several instruments. This led to a lot of confusion as I was told that the things I enjoyed were for girls.

So many boys and girls battle with similar feelings and struggle as they clash with their values, morals, and beliefs. This causes even more distress.

Some people will tell them to claim a new identity — what they feel.

Others will tell them to fight these feelings and suppress them.

For some children, this confusion often centers on attraction to the same sex and they are wondering what they are supposed to do with these feelings. For others, it is a personality quirk. This may become a battle for some as they get older and wonder why they have never had a date or even wanted to go out with someone of the opposite sex. This is real.

Many, many, many preteens and teens will question their sexual identity. Most will settle it quietly and without worry or concern. Some will struggle. Many will be severely affected by these emotions and thoughts.

Help them take these out of the mind — out of the dark — and process them out loud. Many will not want to talk to their parents about this either. This is a critical place to bring in a trusted mentor and friend with a similar biblical sexual ethic who is willing to have these hard conversations on your behalf and offer your child guidance.

Several books have been written that can be of help to youth pastors and teens as they navigate these troubled waters. Do not do this alone. Seek counseling from a trusted, trained Christian counselor. Become knowledgeable by reading the work of those committed to a biblical sexual ethic, or attending conferences or lectures. I highly recommend resources from Godly examples such as **Mark Yarhouse, Preston Sprinkle,** and **Wesley Hill** to families facing these issues.

This is an honest and real struggle.

Do not minimize their questions and the draw of the attraction.

I have found that a powerful tactic to take as a parent or counselor is NOT to negate what they are feeling, but rather lean into the feeling and follow its natural progression. This sounds counter intuitive. Exactly. Listen to that narrative and ask lots of "and then what ..." type questions to help them decide if this is truly a path they want to go down. Then talk about the alternatives. This allows them (and us) to see that there are many paths and it is not always a simple answer. It is complicated. Allow it to be complicated. Be patient.

Remember that in all we do as parents, **we are loving them with the long game in sight.** We want to raise them in the way they should go, but for some, we may not see the fruit today or in the next twenty years. This is a sobering reality.

Encourage them to always seek God's will for themselves by knowing His word. Help them to separate fact from feelings and identify thoughts that are intrusive so that they can consciously and intentionally decide for themselves. I know this sounds like we are talking about a twenty-year-old, but I have had conversations with parents whose children are between the ages of six and ten and are questioning themselves, and their attractions and desires, at this tender age. It happens all too often. Prepare yourselves (and them) for this possibility.

Dignity / Modesty — We are teaching our sons and daughters about modesty and dignity every day and we can be intentional as we make wise decisions.

Let me give you a weird example. We have an Alaskan Malamute that lives in our house. It is wild seeing this monstrous dog all over the house. He is huge. And the hair — it's everywhere! He has free rein in the house, but he does not ever attempt to get on the furniture. The closest he ever gets is to raise a paw from a sitting position. Why? When he was a puppy, we always played with him on the floor. We sat on the floor. He was never picked up and allowed on the bed or furniture. He is bigger now and could hurdle the length of the couch, but he was trained. **This is exactly what we are doing with our children and their future decision making framework. It is being embedded day in and day out from birth.**

Teach your sons and daughters to honor others and themselves — this is dignity.

Modesty reflects the heart.

Help your children grow up aware of the impact of ALL their decisions. Clothing choices. Modesty.

Teach your sons to be respectful regardless of what a girl is wearing.

Teach your daughters when they are young to think ahead. Teach your sons that they are fully responsible for their actions, thoughts, and eyes.

Teach your daughters to honor their brothers with their choice of clothing. This is dignity. This is not popular, yet still so important. We choose how we decide to raise our sons and daughters regarding dignity and modesty, and how those are defined.

Abuse / Trauma — Many parents — more than we realize — must deal with abuse and trauma in their children's lives. The best parents, even those that are aware and involved, will miss something. Harm comes in all shapes and sizes.

How do we prepare our children? You do this by giving them a voice. By giving them tools. We also give them the awareness that even trusted people may not always do good things. This is a hard concept to grasp at this age. **It is the planting of seeds.** Prepare them with skills they need to fight or flee, so that they will not freeze when faced with danger. Run through drills.

We want to prepare our children to say, "NO."

We want our children to have the awareness to see potential harm and flee. Be a force in your children's lives that empowers them to stand up for themselves, and others.

Fear is a terrifying emotion for most of us. Help them to use that energy toward efforts of exposing and rescuing — not silence.

Often parents may miss something with their child due to their own history and the harm they endured, but have not dealt with.

Address these things and you will find you are more intuitive, less cloudy, and more aware of other's intentions. I find that many parents are reactive, undiscerning, and unknowingly contribute to the trauma their child is facing. **I encourage you as strongly as I can to seek help and healing for yourself so that you can be fully available to your family.**

These are weighty matters, but I already feel like you are in a much better place than you were. Now, what about when our children hit the age of eleven plus?

Middle School To High School (11~17)

As a marriage and family counselor that specializes in family, sexuality, gender, and trauma, and in my roles as researcher, professor, speaker, counselor, father, and friend, I have noted an issue that repeatedly comes up and has a HUGE impact on relationships within the family and the choices a pre-teen and teenager makes. This issue is that of **independence**.

If the teen years are entered with complete freedom and zero boundaries, there is a tremendous consequence to that child, their future, and society at large. If this stage of life and development is entered without the freedom to expand, experiment, and grow, they too suffer tremendous consequences which, ironically, are often the same as the young person who had no boundaries.

During their infancy and early years, children need complete care and oversight, which is exhausting. By the time they reach eleven years old though they are capable of doing most things for themselves and of being a help to the family. Some children embrace this independence and are ready to move out as soon as they can. Other children want to linger in childhood and practically insist that they are incapable of meaningful work and we wonder if they will ever leave home.

Problems arise when parents fail to recognize and adjust for how their relationship with their child needs to change. **They must be allowed more freedom and space to make choices. Every child is different and their unique needs and brain development will play into when this hits for your family, but be warned that it will come.**

I tell parents all the time that by the time their son or daughter reaches the age of ten to twelve, their job as a parent (as they know it) is over. I know this is a strong statement and a bit of an exaggeration, but if we do not shift in our approach to our children by this age, in how we interact with them, guide them, and empower them, rebellion is imminent.

Adolescence does not have to be the nightmare so many make it out to be, and what many of us experienced. **Paul David Tripp** calls this life stage an **"age of opportunity."**[30] Why don't we see the fruits of this if it is true?

There are two key reasons that this might be the case.

First, we continue parenting our teenager like we did when they were a nine-year-old.

Second, we did not prepare them well. The truth is that in the pre-teen and teen years we are beginning to see the fruits of the kind of person who developed under our care.

This ought to scare some of us. Thankfully though, it is never too late. **God is a God who is a redeemer.** Rest in this truth.

What we will look at next are key areas we need to help our child navigate. This will look different than how we did it in their elementary years. I hope this life stage can be a beautiful one for you. It will not be for everyone, so hang on for the ride and learn new ways to interact with the pre-adult in your home.

PUBERTY, DATING, GENDER, AND SEXUALITY

Attention! What has your attention? Yes—you, as a parent—what do you spend your time on? Focus. Down time. Wasting time. Compulsions.

What takes your time away, whether intentionally or unintentionally?

How are you as a parent modeling to your children, preteens, and young adults what it means to be a man, woman, husband, wife, employee, friend, listener, enjoyer of life, steward, giver, and child of God?

This life stage invites a whole new world of learning, testing, growing, and forward movement. What demands, captivates, or takes our attention matters.

By age eleven, most of our programming and beliefs are already set in place in our hearts. If we have overloaded our kids with too high of a demand, this sets them up for a fall. If we have limited their experiences, exposure, and they have too much free time, this sets them up to fail. Do you see the theme? We are setting them up for a struggle, an inability to grow up and launch, a lack of skills, grit, work ethic, perseverance, and the vital elements needed to succeed in adulthood. Expect more from them!

Puberty hits soon. Are they prepared for the changes? Help them enter that stage without fear and with anticipation, ready to be a young man or woman that will steward their bodies, sexuality, and gender well.

Through *micro-conversations* and the confidence they gain, your teen can become a leader among their peer group. It is natural at this stage of life for our children to begin pulling way away from us. **We can make this an amazing age of opportunity or a nightmare.** A lot of this will depend on us and our actions as parents, not just our children and their unique personalities.

Dating standards, rules, and a biblical sexual ethic must already be in place by this age. Your child should know what you believe and expect, but also have been allowed to express and test their own ideas.

What kind of husband or wife do they desire one day? This sounds like a crazy question, but remember, parenting as you did when they were younger is over, and we must change our approach with them and even our ways of leading, conversing, and guiding them.

The truth is that for most of our children, their peers and media will have a stronger influence on them than we will from this day forward. Does this scare you? It should. This is why all the previous conversations matter more than ever. Ironically, this is the age that most parents are beginning these conversations ("the talk") — and it is already too late.

Your son's masculinity matters. He is male. How he expresses his masculinity, however, is as different and unique as he is. Stand ready to offer advice, perspective and encouragement for the man God created him to be when his masculinity is challenged by peers or society.

Your daughter's femininity matters. She is female. How she uses, expresses, and lives out her femininity matters. She is unique. She needs permission to feel in her own way, express herself, find herself, and become the woman God created her to be.

Our sons and daughters need clear expressions and boundaries when it comes to gender, its expression and limits. They also need to know we love and care for others that are different than we are — male or female. Stewardship is key.

All that happens now in your child's life is an expression of all that you have invested in them up until now.

If you have been intentional in their early years, then this stage of their life can be an amazing time of growth and maturity.

This means that the teams they play on and how they are treated or mistreated, led, coached, and taught, all matter. The experiences they have at youth group, in school, and other extracurricular activities matter. Signing them up for activities because others are (peer pressure) is not being intentional.

Many families invest heavily into a sport to obtain a scholarship to college. I understand the parents' thoughts. However, many college students that I talk to share that there were other costs along the way. For many, their ideas of masculinity and femininity were shaped by locker room talk and the stress of competition, which led them into eating disorders, promiscuous sexual behaviors, and a loss of other enjoyable activities.

Be intentional and thoughtful as to why you are investing time in any activity for them and what the desired outcome is.

SOCIAL MEDIA AND TECHNOLOGY

I am often asked, **"How do we handle social media and technology with our children?"** It is a quickly changing field and parents are being left behind in the dust. We have a responsibility though to prepare our children to steward this tool well. **I have found that if I think of a smartphone (for example) as a tool and not a toy, it helps me to put it in its rightful place.**

Tools can be a great asset to our life. They make our work quicker and more efficient. Tools, though, can also be misused and cause a great deal of harm. I do not want to get into the weeds of which device is better or which filters will keep your child safe. By the time this book is in your hands that information would be outdated. The purpose and goal here is to give a gentle reminder, a nudge, and some pointers on how to lead our children in this difficult and ever-changing area.

In our day, getting a driver's license was the sign of being grown up. Do you remember how much you looked forward to that day?

Today, the new sign of being grown up is to have a smartphone. And just like a driver's license put us behind the wheel of a powerful machine, the smartphone puts the world — the good and the bad — at our fingertips. Researchers are now reporting more and more ways that smartphones and other forms of technology are detrimental for our brains.

We need to model integrity for our children. Online tools have minimum ages and we should heed that at minimum. Many Christian families lie about their children's birth year to give them access to tools they are not ready to have.

Purposefully decide what your child needs access to — and when they should have that access. Be able to articulate "why" to your teenager. I have known many adolescents who were forbidden access and kept completely away from all forms of technology and this strategy tends to NOT play out well.

One way I have seen actual harm is in how peers at this age interact around topics that they enjoy — video games, movies, smart phone games, and other forms of technology. When they do not have the vocabulary or knowledge to engage with those around them, children often feel isolated, are made fun of, or ignored. On the flipside, though, many young people are harmed by bullying via text, a social media post, email, or a video that disappears. There is potential danger on both sides of this equation. Be aware. Be vigilant. Have *micro-conversations*. These hopefully began when they were younger, but they are different now. Now the depth increases. Your honesty and vulnerability increases. Their independence is imminent. You have a young adult in the making.

What you watch, whether streaming or a movie, are key opportunities — tools for these *micro-conversations*. Dive in. Use pivotal, awkward scenes as the springboard for deeper *micro-conversations*. Discuss what happened between the characters. Ask if they have ever experienced something similar. Continue to prepare and build into the young adult in your home so that they can make decisions for themselves, and learn boundaries with movies and what they consume.

Remember the goal of parenting is NOT just protection, it is about preparation, and your child's heart.

STEWARDSHIP AND YOUR CHILD'S HEART

Your son or daughter is now a young adult. They are grown up. They are out on their own, or in college. What are the decisions they are facing now? What are the pressures and temptations?

The key word for success is "stewardship."

We are responsible for our children, but the responsibility begins to shift to our teen as they prepare to leave the nest.

Their responsibility has been increasing over the years, and at the same time, our responsibility and supervision decreases. We are playing the long game here. We want to see the results of heart change, not just behavior. This is played out in the recesses of their minds, and hearts, as they navigate big decisions, attractions, and temptations.

As they mature, their attractions naturally grow. Their sexuality, hormones, and feelings become a force to be reckoned with. Masturbation, pornography and other forms of escape become even more enticing and alluring. Every decision they make impacts their future.

Our role is to provide guardrails that keep them on the road. As they first start driving, they may hit the shoulder and come up against that guardrail. Over time though they can drive safely down the road, thankful that the guardrails were in place when they were learning, but are not something they depend on daily to stay on the road. This day will come sooner for some than others, but we are all individuals and mature at our own pace.

What if your son or daughter became a leader that helped others make wise decisions and overcome past choices and traumas?

What if they encouraged others to lead a life that honored the God of the Bible? This would be incredible. Set this dream before them. They can be huge change agents in the lives of those around them. Everyone influences someone.

If you have modeled redemptive speech in your conversations with your child, they are more likely to speak with compassion to others. As they steward their sexuality, treating people that they meet with respect will stand out in the crowd and provide an opportunity to share about a God who loves them and designed them with a purpose.

CHAPTER 5

QUESTIONS ABOUT GENDER, HOMOSEXUALITY, AND SAME-SEX ATTRACTION

Many of us wish that we could steer clear of these difficult topics and go back to a day when issues of sexuality were more simple. To be honest though, those days never existed. In "those" days the culture and the church were not forgiving, gracious, or understanding with those truly fighting internal battles over their gender and attractions. These are real fights. Today these battles are still fought internally, but those fighting are encouraged to go public with their battle or give up on the battle altogether. Men and women are encouraged to surrender to whatever feeling is strongest at the moment and claim that as an identity.

We have a responsibility to our children and their future to address the critical issues of gender, homosexuality, and same-sex attraction from a biblical perspective and with grace and compassion through *micro-conversations*. **This chapter is a stepping stone for you as a parent as you help your children develop their own ethic, or ETHOS, based on biblical truth, scientific evidence, and grace, at a young age.**

Do you have a theology and framework — an understanding — that will allow you to share with your children the beauty and intricacies of male and female, masculinity and femininity, and gender?

Is it a simple binary belief (male or female) — with only two options?

Or is it filled with the intricacy, differences, and beauty with which God created every one of us — in His image?

What are your theological, personal and familial attitudes, conversations, and even jokes surrounding homosexuality and same-sex attraction?

We must be prepared to manage these *micro-conversations* with our families well and early.

Much of your children's sexual ethic is established early on through observation of the world around them and personal experience.

Be a source of intentional teaching and education for them. Today, gender questions are an important part of growing up.

Homosexuality and your beliefs, attitudes, and sensitivity matters.

Understanding same-sex attraction is critical for us as parents so that we can lead well.

Gender Questions

I am not surprised by the gender questions that are filling the airwaves today. When most of us were growing up, some of these same questions being asked by your peers or family were beginning to buck traditional gender roles. Women were working more outside the home and men were helping around the house. Others were asking why they should look or act a certain way or enjoy certain things simply because they were a boy or a girl. Boys grew their hair long and pierced their ears. Girls cut their hair and joined the football team. This was and is quite normal.

The reality today is that we just hear about it more vocally than ever before. This is not new. Some pre-adolescents and adolescents wrestle with who they are when they don't fit the stereotypes. Statistically though, most will not give this issue much thought if left to themselves. We are seeing this issue surrounded by extreme rhetoric and even violence. This is the world today, so how do we engage our children in conversations that enable them to be confident and secure in who God created them to be?

Genesis 1:27 says:
> "So God created human beings in his own image. In the image of God he created them; male and female he created them" (NLT).

The follow up to the creation of two genders is the bringing together of the two in Genesis 2:18:
> "Then the Lord God said, 'It is not good for the man to be alone. I will make a helper who is just right for him'" (NLT).

Verse 23 says:
> "'At last!' the man exclaimed. 'This is bone of my bone, and flesh from my flesh! She will be called "woman,"

because she was taken from "man"'" (NLT).

Then came the creation of the place these two were united as one. Verse 24 says:
"This explains why a man leaves his father and mother and is joined to his wife, and the two are united into one" (NLT).

Verse 25 takes one step further:
"Now the man and his wife were both naked, but they felt no shame" (NLT).

BOY—MAN——MASCULINITY

First off, I want to clearly state that the idea of two genders — and **only two genders** — is not a mistake. It is by God's design. What you believe about that will shape how you lead your child. We are born male or female. A small number of people are born with ambiguous genitalia and this creates a lot of difficulty for their parents and later the young person in knowing who they are. These families need incredible support and biblical counsel. The decisions to be made are also never simple.

Others are clearly born either male or female and this is determined in the womb. How this plays out individually is a different story. How you personally relate to your masculinity or femininity matters. But even more important in our psyche is how we relate to the image of who we think we are supposed to be.

My personal development was filled with angst, confusion, frustration, and questions — with no answers. This led to disturbing self-beliefs and even hatred, and this is not uncommon. No one knew that I was struggling — I told no one. I've learned that as parents we need to engage in these conversations with our sons and daughters because they most likely will not bring it up on their own.

We need to give them permission to verbalize and process ideas, questions, feelings, frustrations, and even their opposition.

They need to know it is okay to process ideas they have heard elsewhere. You need to be a safe place for this to occur, or secure a safe place for them to ask these questions in a healthy biblical community, with a Christian counselor, or even a trusted mentor. **Don't do this alone, but remember that you are the one on the front lines with your children.**

Where do these conversations start? With you.

Do not wait for them to ask.

Do not wait for them to bring it up.

Engage daily in *micro-conversations* that draw them to a healthy self-awareness, identity, and a biblical sexual ethic.

I am listening to music on YouTube right now as I write and a video has popped up as an advertisement stating we need to ditch the definition of masculinity and "#EvolveTheDefinition."[31]

I do agree, to a point. Why is this so complicated? It seems like it should be obvious, but for many, it is not clear.

So, what is the problem? How we define 'male,' 'men,' and 'masculine' needs a framework. The definition of 'woman,' 'female,' and 'femininity' needs some boundaries. This is a critical point. These frameworks and boundaries are driven by our family culture, our church culture, and the wider culture of the country that we live in. If we were to go to the average sitcom or T.V. drama for our definition of masculinity, we would see one of two extremes usually portrayed. Sitcoms portray men as weak, submissive, powerless, and foolish. Dramas tend to portray men as violent, angry, sexually aggressive, and selfish.

Do you want your daughter to marry a man like these shows portray?

In his book *Boys Adrift* (2007), **Dr. Leonard Sax**[32] states that five factors are driving the growing epidemic of unmotivated boys and underachieving young men.

He first identifies the **changes in our school systems** over the years that have hindered boys' ability to learn as they fail to acknowledge that they have different needs than girls.

The second factor is **excessive video game play**.

The third factor is **ADHD medications.**

The fourth factor is **endocrine disruptors**—hormones in beef, plastics, and the like that are impacting our children and their physical and sexual development. Boys are being hormonally feminized and girls are starting their periods and developing at a younger age, which he then connects to their failure to launch into adulthood—a culture of lazy adult men.

Lastly, Dr. Sax identifies the fifth culprit as **a loss of positive role models**.

So, what are the solutions and a framework for masculinity?

Some solutions presented by Dr. Sax were to challenge the traditional K–12 educational system. It does not promote growth and health in boys. Parents, this is a call for you to be involved in your children's schools and be a change agent for your children and other children's futures.

Second, give your sons opportunities to engage in the real world so that there is a decrease in the need for the fake world of video games. This is the heart of the problem with video games. It is not the games in themselves, but the replacement of real world interactions.

Third, be educated on medications for ADHD and their long-term effects. Check out **Dr. Daniel Amen's** book *Healing ADD*[33] in which he discusses the seven types of ADD. There is no one simple diagnosis with one treatment that works for everyone. He also provides suggestions for alternatives to try prior to medication.

Fourth, research and be aware of environmental estrogens and the impact of these on your son's growth and development.

Finally, and most importantly, you need to be sure your son has positive role models. They need strong, consistent examples of what it means to be a man, and what masculinity is.

The advertisement I mentioned seeing on YouTube, stating that we need to redefine masculinity and "#EvolveTheDefinition,"[34] raises some questions.

For many, when they think of masculinity, their experience leads them to associate it with negative stereotypes of foolishness or aggression. And it is right to challenge these stereotypes and their damaging expression in our sons.

What are your son and daughter being taught about masculinity in your home?
What can you do to intentionally teach your sons and daughters about masculinity?

Is it okay for a boy to learn that taking care of others before himself is an honorable thing to do, or is this sexist and gender stereotyping?

It is important for you to think through these things as you study the Bible and lead your family into a biblical sexual ethic.

Dr. Philip Zimbardo, a well-known psychologist and researcher, has written a book called *The Demise of Guys* (2012)[35] and has an excellent TED talk on the subject as well.

The **three factors** he identified for the demise are
1. pornography,
2. excessive video game play, and
3. absent fathers.

What can we do with this data as we think through mentoring and discipling the boys growing up in our homes?

The first thing we should do is teach them about pornography — its allure and danger. This is NOT a one-time conversation — rather, it is a thousand *micro-conversations* that plant the seeds and thoughts of an intentional ETHOS in our sons' minds. **If we do not have these *micro-conversations*, someone else will, if they are not already.**

We need to limit video game play and encourage and reward real-world engagement.

We make sure they are employed as soon as they are legally able. We teach and model a healthy work ethic.

We encourage dreams, passions, and interests that promote them getting outside of themselves and into the lives of others. Video games are often a selfish escape to avoid relationships with others.

We teach them an ETHOS of time management, relationship engagement, and investment in others.

Dads — we need to be engaged with our children. We are the leaders, whether we want to be or not. Be a positive example in how you talk to and treat your wife. If you are a single mom or a mother parenting with a disengaged husband, you need to **intentionally seek out healthy male role models for your son to spend time with.**

So much of our children's future is dependent on our sons having a healthy, biblically sound understanding of masculinity.

It is NOT aggressive, but can be assertive when it needs to be.

It is NEVER domineering, but is a servant leader with a voice, vision, passion, and insight.

What else would you add to a definition of masculinity?

Spend some time in prayer and studying Scripture for yourself to see the characteristics of a man that the Lord boasts of and teach and model these characteristics to your children.

Have *micro-conversations* often about the sort of man you hope he will be, or the sort of man you would want your daughter to partner with for life.

GIRL—WOMAN—FEMININITY

How would you define femininity and womanhood?

Would your description include their bodies, personalities, actions, or character?

Which should it be? Do you think of cooking and cleaning, pornography, empowerment, or something else?

Your definition matters.

My goal here is to expose some of your ways of thinking as a mom or dad about womanhood and femininity, so that you can lead with intentionality and forethought. Much of what occurs today in conversation about femininity is not well thought through and is reactionary. Some is abusive and offensive. I am saddened as a father and husband by the narrowing definition of identity centered on their body. The church's definition has not been much better, when it limits women with a strict definition linked solely to a woman's role as wife, mother, and homemaker.

How do we counteract this as parents of daughters and sons who will be marrying one day?

Girls compare themselves to others and wonder, "Am I good enough, pretty enough, smart enough, tough enough, etc."

Our daughters are at risk, just as much as our sons. They have so much against them, but the most powerful forces at work are the battles in their own minds. **Nancy Leigh DeMoss** writes in *Lies Women Believe* (2001)[36] that listening to the lying serpent leads down a slippery slope of disobedience. The truth is that what you believe matters. Who you listen to matters. This is critical as we raise our daughters.

Who is speaking into her life, giving her value, identity, courage, and strength besides you?

Our ETHOS as parents matters because we are leading them to develop their own ETHOS from a place of truth, not lies. Think about your own story and how the lies you believed and were exposed to at some time in your life impacted how you view God, yourself, sin, marriage, children, emotions, and your circumstances. We want out daughters' foundational beliefs about themselves and their bodies to be based on TRUTH and not the lies she may be tempted to believe.

This is only the tip of the iceberg. **Dr. Daniel Amen** discusses the uniqueness of women in his book *Unleash the Power of the Female Brain* (2013).[37]

Men and women are vastly different, and this is a good thing. As we discover more about neurobiology — a fascinating field of study — the complexity and brilliance of God's design of the sexes becomes apparent. Women have assets in their minds that men do not possess. They also have liabilities. Through our *micro-conversations* with a daughter, we want to encourage her to understand herself — her unique intuition, her ability to empathize and collaborate, and her self-control.

We should educate our daughters on the complexity of the endocrine system and that the food she eats, her exposure to toxins, and the fluctuating hormones in her body will affect her mood and outlook on life. She will battle addictions, anxiety, and the comparison trap.

Your daughter's social connectedness is a powerful tool—and it can be both an asset and a liability. Each of our daughters were uniquely knit in their mother's womb. Some are impulsive, and others are compulsive. Some lean toward sadness or anxiety. Preparing your daughter to know herself and providing her with the tools she will need is a critical part of raising a young woman into adulthood.

In *Why Gender Matters* (2005) **Dr. Leonard Sax**[38] demonstrates that boys and girls are different. The better we understand these differences, the more free we are to be ourselves. This is taught in the home, modeled, and lived out. He shares an example that when asked to draw a picture, **girls typically draw nouns** (people, places, or things) and **boys draw verbs** (actions, states, or occurrences).

As girls mature, changes in their brains' activity move emotions out of the **amygdala** into the **cerebral cortex**, while boys' emotions remain in the **amygdala**.

Dr. Sax is critical of the idea that boys need "emotional literacy" and should talk more about their feelings.

This displays a lack of understanding or care that boys and girls are biologically different in many areas and that we should not force them to be the same.

Dr. Sax states, "You are asking [a boy] to make connections between two parts of his brain that don't normally communicate."[39] We are different.

How can you help your daughter celebrate these differences and embrace them?

What do your daughters need from you?

They need your strong influence in their earlier years—birth to ten—but then the freedom to wrestle with ideas as they get older.

Think about it this way: **You have approximately ten years to speak into your daughter's life as her primary influence.** After that, life changes drastically. Our daughters are vulnerable and many of us are unwilling to engage in the hard conversations needed before they are twelve or fourteen.

By the time they are in their pre-teen years, they are much more interested in what their peers and the media say than what you say.

It is never too late, but your tactics and approach MUST change after they reach the age of eleven, though this age varies between children.

Over the years, what you have voiced as **beautiful** influences what she will see as **beautiful**.

When you complain about your body, its shape, or that of your spouse, your daughter's opinions are being formed.

This affects what they see as negative, unwanted, or unacceptable. The discussions you have driving around town influence them. Have you ever heard your child making a comment verbally that sounds offensive — even downright mean — yet you immediately realize that they are only repeating something they have heard you say? That's painful. They are little sponges and mirrors. This is why the *micro-conversations* we have with them **PRIOR to puberty** matter more than almost any of the others we will have with them during their teenage years.

Are you prepared?

The truth regarding gender is that it is NOT as simple as "boy" or "girl."
That aspect is almost always clear and determined by biology. As the young child in Kindergarten Cop told us, "Boys have a penis. Girls have a vagina." And both genders come with their own limitations, despite what the world seems to be telling children, and each child will have their own limitations. We can live within these and find amazing freedom, or fight them our entire life and live a very frustrated and angry existence.

PARENTS — TO DO!

Last night, I was sitting outside with my twelve-year-old son after an eight-mile bicycle ride through Salem, Oregon. We discussed girls, dating, and marriage, but our conversation also ranged to peer pressure — the fear of walking into a room and not knowing where to sit, and the stress of the weight of others' opinions about us. All of this was initiated by him, not me. I followed where the topics went.

How did this happen? A million *micro-conversations* have been the theme of our home and have created a foundation — an ETHOS — that gave him the confidence to be vulnerable.

I tell my children, even before puberty, that they are their own person and make their own decisions, and, thus, are fully responsible for those decisions. This matters as we prepare them to bear the weight of more difficult decisions and their consequences.

If they forget to take something to school or camp, and you come bail them out, what are they learning? Are they learning responsibility, or that others will cover for them? Do we let small mistakes shape them, so they can avoid the larger ones down the road?

Do you anticipate the teenage years to be full of conflict, or of excitement, as you see that they can be trusted to use wisdom as they make choices regarding their sexuality, dating, and relationship boundaries?

Prepare a list of the character qualities and skills you want to see in your sons and/or your daughters when they leave your home. List ideas for how to prepare your child to meet these goals.

Have a conversation with your son or daughter about what qualities they (and you) believe are important in themselves, their friends, and the opposite sex. What boundaries in dating need to be established before their heart is involved?

Homosexuality

A distraught young woman came into my office needing advice and some direction. She believed that since she was in a lesbian relationship and I was a Christian, I would condemn her for her behavior. She assumed I would be like a parent, but instead, I asked her for more details.

I asked her explicitly how the physical parts of her relationship were going. She looked confused.

I asked her if she felt safe with this person. She said yes. I asked her if touch was wonderful. She said, "Yes."

I asked her if being close was intoxicating. She said, "Oh yes!" She was confused as to where I was going with this, as it was the opposite direction of where she had expected me to go.

I then asked her why she was here — why did she feel guilt and shame? She declared it was because she knew, despite her feelings, that her behavior was wrong.

I asked her again how she expected me to help her. She was stuck. She knew that a lesbian relationship was not God's designed place for this kind of sexual expression. Sexual touch is a delicate balance.

The reality is that the touch of a person who has been deemed safe can invigorate and feel good as the dopamine release increases. However, the same kind of look and touch by another person destroys our soul, crushes us, and is harmful.

God designed our sexuality with purpose (the three P's). It is also meant to be stewarded and has consequences. This young woman knew what she needed to do. She knew her heart's desire.

The other big question though, for her was, "Who am I?" What are the labels we use today? Gay, lesbian, bisexual, etc. The last time I looked, Facebook had added 52+ options for gender.

We are all looking for similar things — to be known, to be loved, to be accepted, to belong, and to be somebody.

Anyone that helps us answer these longings becomes our savior. This is a dangerous role for any human to play.

I helped this young woman in my office understand that what she felt was normal.

I helped her see that her desire for love, intimacy, security, and to be known, were good, God-given, and beautiful.

I helped her see that touch is amazing, especially when received from someone you consider safe.

I also helped her see that she had value and did not have to be driven by whatever made her feel good in the moment, but could be guided by a biblical sexual ethic. If she had had an ETHOS grounded in Scripture, it is much easier to resist the temporary high of attraction. The wounds from her family of origin were tremendous. Her wounds from men were heartbreaking. These were overcome with counseling. But her identity, by choice, is in Christ, and who He created her to be. Today, she is single and is a faithful servant in ministry.

Approximately fourteen years ago I had been counseling for several years in churches and in private practice when I entered the academic world as a professor. I was now working with more college age students than I had previously and saw that most of them believed that "love" — feelings and emotions — trump truth — both God's revealed truth and biology.

In years past, the church reacted to sexual choices that were outside of God's design with criticism and anger, not redemption and compassion. A lot has changed over the years. One of the consequences, though, of the church's growth in compassion and understanding has been that young adults now increasingly believe that everyone should make up their own mind as to what makes them happy and embrace it — whatever it is.

The sexual ethic of Christians is the weakest it has ever been in recent history as the call to love our neighbor was not accompanied by teaching on healthy sexuality in our homes and churches.

I want us, as parents, to equip our children so that they can address these complicated issues with **compassion**, biblical truth, and a servant's heart. My hope is that we will raise a generation that knows that **the gospel is for everyone** — just as they are.

The power of the gospel is that it transforms.

We were never meant to stay where we were when Christ saved us.
We are meant to be challenged, to do hard things, and to give up idols and even some relationships we may desire — for the sake of the gospel.

We must die to ourselves in order to live. This is critical. This is compelling. Thank God for grace!

A BRIEF HISTORY

A quote commonly attributed to Dietrich Bonhoeffer (although the source is actually unknown) says,
"The ultimate test of a moral society is the kind of world that it leaves to its children."

The reality is that there have always been men and women that were same-sex attracted, and others that were asexual, throughout history. We have always had men and women that questioned their sexuality. The difference today is that this is all being done in a much more public manner in the U.S. and in many other countries. There is also a trend to classify the words of anyone that speaks out against the behaviors of the LGBTQ+ (Lesbian, Gay, Bisexual, Transgender. Queer/Questioning+) community as hate speech and illegal. I want to equip you, as a parent, to understand more of these issues and then you can lead your sons and daughters in an understanding of a biblical sexual ethic, and how to respond to others in a way that honors Christ.

In recent years, bullying has been highlighted — rightly so — as a problem among children and teenagers, but with a bent toward protecting LGBTQ students. I want you to think about this. Is this wrong? NO! No one should be bullied. However, there is a twist. While it may have started with protecting and normalizing LGBTQ students, it has morphed into embracing and encouraging these behaviors. This is a critical shift.

There are only two options today for a church:
- to embrace and encourage or
- to be considered haters.

How did we get here? There have been strategic shifts in our culture and the language used. An example of this was the push in the 1990s of the idea that we are all "born this way."

The reality is that a few weeks after gay marriage was legalized the shift in the conversation was to gender fluidity. That is where we are now—you choose. You aren't, in fact, "born this way." Let your child born today decide if they want to be a boy or girl. Who are we to tell them? This is a terrifying stance with grave consequences.

Many churches have been pushed into a corner and in order to avoid the label of "hate group" have defaulted to embracing and affirming sexual behaviors that Scripture warns against. There is no middle ground left.

Queer theology says that you are made in the image of God — your identity matters. You should embrace what you feel, since God does not make mistakes. Your desires are made by God and of God, so they must be good and acted upon. Everything is about you — not God or His Son. There is no discipleship or dying to self. Marriage is mocked and families are divided.

I fear for our young people, whether they are Christian or not. They have a battle before them to reclaim a view of masculinity and femininity as God designed—not one that says girl = pink, boy = blue, or that girls bake and boys are athletes. NO!

A biblical view of masculinity and femininity has both sexes honoring and complementing the other, supporting the other. Each person embraces their complete self — faults and all — for the glory of God.

REAL PEOPLE WE LOVE

Your ETHOS — what you believe and live out — matters.

How you discuss and live out gender matters.

In my marriage, one of us is very sensitive, emotional, processes everything they are thinking out loud, and even cries with commercials. The other one of us is quiet, introspective, analytical, skeptical, a fighter, and an internal processor that does not like to share emotions.

Which one am I? Which one is my wife?

Many readers will likely fall into stereotypes and quickly assume that the first one is my wife. You would be wrong though! I cry every time at the end of the movie "Cars." I am the "girl" in my marriage. Or, should we perhaps challenge our assumptions about gender and recognize that both men and women represent the full spectrum of human behavior, thought, and emotion. I am the emotional one. I am the external and verbal processor. I cry at almost every movie. But, I can also fix almost anything in a house or car, and have a healthy male sex drive. We have a lot of work to do to expand — maybe better said, to deepen — these definitions, not rewrite them.

The truth is that most men are not "manning up" and showing themselves to be someone of strength, character, leadership, with a work ethic, and tender and protective of others. Women are being used, abused and discounted just as often today as they were in the past. We have serious inequities. Our actions reveal what we believe as healthy, normal, good, right, and biblical. **So many of the things we wrestle with, though, do not have chapter and verse answers in Scripture, which leads us to more questions.**

This is not about knowing whether your son liking pink or your daughter enjoying getting muddy is okay. It is much deeper than that. This is where we get the word identity. Who am I?

We are all looking for something. We all want to be desired, known, to have worth, or to accomplish something. Somewhere along the way, though, a key part of who we are, our sexuality, gets messed with in the process. **Without a guiding principle as to why you should or should not do something, decisions become arbitrary.**

We must start with laying a foundation. As we begin, I want to clearly state that by God's design you are born as either male or female. This is not radical. It is deciding to place my starting point in biological facts that I ascribe to God as His prerogative as the Creator. You and I had no say in the matter when the hormone bath in-utero made each of us male or female. This is a foundation.

What is your foundation for creating a biblical sexual ethic?

For many, the foundation is tradition. We love or hate the things we do because that is the way our family has always done it. **We hold views that are entrenched in tradition— not the Bible.**

So, what will your foundation be as you teach and lead your children intentionally?

Homosexuality is a reality today just as it was throughout all of time. This is not a new thing. Some societies have embraced it, while others demonized it.

The reality, as you know in your heart, is that **we are not talking about an issue — we are talking about people.** We are talking about hurting people, who are just like us. You and I are desiring and deeply yearning for something. Some reason that we should not deny people anything that makes them happy. That argument falls to pieces, though, when we insert anything else that may potentially be harmful in the place of homosexual sex. People find happiness in all sorts of places— with people, with animals, with sports, with hobbies. That is not the purpose of this book though. **I want us to know how to teach our children compassion and a biblical response.**

The majority of the LGBTQ+ conversations center around the individual and their feelings. **I would dare say that the gospel asks us to die to ourselves and our families and live for Christ.** Am I willing to sign up for that? Are you? This requires us to choose things we might not want to choose for the sake of a greater call on our lives. This requires sacrifice, loneliness, and suffering. Ironically, in our talk of self-denial, we are getting closer to the example of the life of Christ.

God has a perfect design for sex and intercourse, and that is in a heterosexual marriage. Teaching this to our children is critical. Living this out is imperative. We also need to explain to our children why we believe as we do, so that they can in turn, lead others toward good things, not condemn them. We ought to be full of love, grace, compassion, care — even worry — and then reach out a helping hand and be patient for God to do His work in the lives of those we are serving, in His time, and in His manner. We are just called to be faithful. Your theology matters. Your beliefs about homosexuality matter.

What does Scripture say about homosexuality?

There are five passages that specifically mention homosexuality. Personally, what I have found is that these Scripture passages are quickly twisted and manipulated to mean different things than a traditional evangelical ethic. At this point using these passages for any debate or argument becomes difficult. **What I personally choose to do is to stick to a biblical sexual ethic in a more general sense.** Scripture clearly limits sexual relationships to one single place — between a man and a woman within the committed marriage bed.

There is no other place for genital sexual expression. This confirms a sexual ethic that answers questions about homosexuality. Genital sexual experiences are never permissible with the same sex.

The passages on homosexuality are:

Leviticus 18:22 and 20:13 clearly condemns homosexuality.

Romans 1:26–27 prohibits same-sex behavior.

1 Corinthians 6:9–10 and 1 Timothy 1:9–10 mention same-sex sexual behavior.

PARENTS — TO DO!

Teach your children about God's design for marriage, sex, and family.

Be an example when you fail by asking for forgiveness.

Be an example when others fail and you forgive them and help them up.

Be careful in your speech as you raise your children. They ARE listening, and they are absorbing your attitudes, angers, and fears. **They know what you really think about people.**

Ask your children questions and challenge them to think deeper on subjects. It is okay for them to wrestle with a question for awhile and develop an answer later.

Give your children hope by speaking positively about their future, our world, society, and people. Cynicism cuts to the heart.

Invite your children to face challenges that are a struggle for them and in which they might even fail. Pick them up, dust them off, and lead them on. While they are between the shaping ages of birth and ten, be intentional.

After they reach their teens, prepare to step back and know that you will hurt more. Prepare to let go — slowly, intentionally, thoughtfully — as you give them more room.

Observe them interacting with the world through the lens you purposefully crafted over the years. This is critical for your eleven-year-old. And your twelve-year-old. And your thirteen-year-old.

Many of them will already have the tendency to pull away by then — let them. Be hopeful and proud of the young man or woman they are becoming. Be a breath of fresh air in their lives as they navigate the teenage years — not a source of tension. They will have enough of that out in the world. **Make your home a safe place — for them, and for yourself.**

Are you getting excited about the potential? Make it happen. How? **Intentionally help them develop their ETHOS young, so that they are living by it by age eleven. You can do this.**

A biblical sexual ethic rests in scriptures such as these:

Naked and Unashamed — Genesis 2:24–25
"This explains why a man leaves his father and mother and is joined to his wife, and the two are united into one. Now the man and his wife were both naked, but they felt no shame" (NLT).

Her Breasts — Proverbs 5:19:
"She is a loving deer, a graceful doe. Let her breasts satisfy you always. May you always be captivated by her love" (NLT).

Lust = Adultery — Matthew 5:28:
"But I say, anyone who even looks at a woman with lust has already committed adultery with her in his heart" (NLT).

Become One Flesh — Matthew 19:4-6:
"Haven't you read," he replied, "that at the beginning the Creator 'made them male and female,' and said, 'For this reason a man will leave his father and mother and be united to his wife, and the two will become one flesh'? So they are no longer two, but one flesh. Therefore what God has joined together, let no one separate." (NIV).

Remain Single — Better to Marry than to Burn —
1 Corinthians 7:8–9:

"Now to the unmarried and the widows I say: It is good for them to stay unmarried, as I do. But if they cannot control themselves, they should marry, for it is better to marry than to burn with passion" (NIV).

Sexual Immorality—Mathew 15:19:

"For from the heart come evil thoughts, murder, adultery, all sexual immorality, theft, lying, and slander" (NLT).

Acts 15:19–20:

"It is my judgment, therefore, that we should not make it difficult for the Gentiles who are turning to God. Instead we should write to them, telling them to abstain from food polluted by idols, from sexual immorality..." (NIV).

1 Corinthians 6:18–20:

"Run from sexual sin! No other sin so clearly affects the body as this one does. For sexual immorality is a sin against your own body. Don't you realize that your body is the temple of the Holy Spirit, who lives in you and was given to you by God? You do not belong to yourself, for God bought you with a high price. So you must honor God with your body" (NLT).

1 Corinthians 7:2–7:

"But since sexual immorality is occurring, each man should have sexual relations with his own wife, and each woman with her own husband. The husband should fulfill his marital duty to his wife, and likewise the wife to her husband. The wife does not have authority over her own body but yields it to her husband. In the same way, the husband does not have authority over his own body but yields it to his wife. Do not deprive each other except perhaps by mutual consent and for a time, so that you may devote yourselves to prayer. Then come together again so that Satan will not tempt you because of your lack of self-control. I say this as a concession, not as a command. I wish that all of you were as I am. But each of you has your own gift from God; one has this gift, another has that" (NIV).

Galatians 5:19–21:
"When you follow the desires of your sinful nature, the results are very clear: sexual immorality, impurity, lustful pleasures, idolatry, sorcery, hostility, quarreling, jealousy, outbursts of anger, selfish ambition, dissension, division, envy, drunkenness, wild parties, and other sins like these. Let me tell you again, as I have before, that anyone living that sort of life will not inherit the Kingdom of God" (NLT).

Colossians 3:5:
"So put to death the sinful, earthly things lurking within you. Have nothing to do with sexual immorality, impurity, lust, and evil desires. Don't be greedy, for a greedy person is an idolater, worshiping the things of this world" (NLT).

1 Thessalonians 4:3–5:
"God's will is for you to be holy, so stay away from all sexual sin. Then each of you will control his own body and live in holiness and honor—not in lustful passion like the pagans who do not know God and his ways" (NLT).

Hebrews 13:4.
"Give honor to marriage, and remain faithful to one another in marriage. God will surely judge people who are immoral and those who commit adultery" (NLT).

Same-Sex Attraction

Jeff finds himself feeling that he is not much of a sexual being at the age of twenty. He is active and works and has friends, but has never had a girlfriend and always wondered if something was wrong. He has always been attracted to guys, but it has not necessarily been a sexual thing either.

Phil is fifteen and has no interest in dating girls. He is attracted to men that give him attention and value. He is a Christian and confused as to what to do with these feelings that everyone around him seems to say are wrong. Should he be in a same-sex relationship, and eventually get married? Deny his feelings? Embrace them? Be disgusted by them?

Janice has always dreamed of being married and a big wedding. Now, at the age of seventeen, she finds herself very interested in girls in her life and completely turned off by all the boys her age. What does this mean?

Pam is an attractive athlete — confident, a leader with a strong personality. She never dreamed of being attracted to girls. She is now twenty-one and not interested in marriage like her friends seem to be. She had a brief sexual experience with an older woman a few years earlier and is now very confused about her feelings today. "Am I gay? Am I broken? Am I okay? Is this okay?" She is quite lost.

Same-sex attraction was not talked about much in years past. Today, it is a topic of conversation everywhere. Is it normal? Some research points out that more than twenty-five percent of adolescents will struggle with their sexual identity during their teenage years, and most of them will foreclose on this struggle by claiming a heterosexual identity.[40]

The struggle is a normal part of growing up. **Dr. Mark Yarhouse**, a Christian researcher, added framework to the discussion years ago through his scholarship and teaching. Many people that identify themselves as gay are probably more accurately placed in the space of being same-sex attracted. What does this mean? They are attracted to the same-sex, but are not claiming a gay identity. Though "same-sex attracted" and "gay identity" may sound synonymous, they are not.

By adding this framework, it **creates a space to wrestle** and admit to a struggle without having to claim an identity. This has led many people — particularly young people — into a deeper understanding of themselves, the appropriate amount of weight they need to put on their feelings and attractions, and the complexity of who they are. This is a space we desperately need.

For some of us, our children are going to go through this struggle. A word of caution — be careful about how you love and encourage them in this process. They probably already know your thoughts, opinions and judgments regarding homosexuality. They do not need that. **They need space, questions, care, touch, and leadership.** You will hopefully still have permission to lead them — at least somewhat — so take what you can at this stage. Prayerfully walk with them, offering guidance through these struggles and questions.

I would encourage you to read the thoughtful books written by **Dr. Mark Yarhouse**[41] and **Dr. Preston Sprinkle**[42] for a compassionate Christian viewpoint.

Identity struggles are real. The strength of attractions can be overwhelming. I could take the time here to describe the research and findings on the various aspects of the debate on same-sex attraction, but I prefer to focus on the hearts of our children.

Every parent will do some harm to their children. Yes, even you. I have spoken harshly at times and caused harm. I was too soft when they needed strength, and caused harm. This is a reality of the fallen world we live in.

Dr. Dan Allender[43] describes a hunger that grows in all of us as we mature and prepare to leave our father and mother. Why? **We cannot be all things to our children.**

Most parents seem unwilling to embrace this reality. Once we do embrace it though, there is great freedom as we realize we do not have to strive for perfection. When we fail, we get to model seeking forgiveness and restoring the relationship. They get an opportunity to practice forgiveness. A lot of the wrestling and struggles our children will go through are due to who we are as parents. I know some of you will blame yourselves for your children's mistakes for the rest of your lives. That is too far though. They have free will, and share the responsibility. Others, though, are unaware, or unable to admit to the impact they have on their children and their development.

Do you and your family spend a lot of time out with other people in social settings? One child may thrive in this environment and their personality benefit from a social setting.
Another child may shrink back in the face of crowds and learn to loathe social situations.

Is your family active or sedentary? This impacts your children.

Do you eat a healthy, balanced diet, or do you eat poorly? Are you a good example for healthy eating and living? This impacts our children.

Are you and your spouse openly affectionate in front of your children? This has a huge impact on your child's sense of security — even if they act like it is gross.

The energy and culture of your home has a tremendous impact on your child's physical development, spiritual formation, and sense of security.

A THEOLOGY

So, let me go to a question I hear a lot.

Is attraction to the same sex sin? Let's unpack attraction. I personally believe we have such a distorted view of attraction that it confuses a lot of our life choices. It is critical we have this in the right place, not only for those who feel a same-sex attraction, but also those that are attracted to the opposite sex.

Do you have control of your attractions?

Can you see someone and control whether you think they are "good-looking" or not?

Do you have the ability to NOT be aroused by someone that you deem attractive?

Is arousal sin?
Some would place this under the umbrella of self-control. I disagree though. The men and women I know that have learned the art and skill of "controlling" their attractions and what arouses them are not doing well and face different challenges and difficulties. They marry one day and are unable to "turn on" what they successfully conquered, controlled, and "turned off." **This is not stewardship.**

What breaks my heart is that we would very likely parade this young man or woman around as the picture of the perfect young Christian — "self-controlled." I would say emphatically — NO! They are not quite human. **That is NOT stewardship.**

It is more like a denial or a dismissal of a part of God's perfect design, stating it is flawed and bad — maybe even evil. No, No, NO! **Stewardship is the key.** You and I have feelings and attractions and experience arousal that we must learn to correctly value.

The data we receive in our brains based on attraction, feelings, desires, and arousal is subjective. **Parents, how are you stewarding your sexual attractions?** Think about what happens when this data is a larger chunk of someone's identity and it is telling them something different than everyone else around them. This is a confusing space. **This is that space where that person needs us the most.**

They need a place to ask questions, to feel, to hurt, and even to grieve. A key aspect of having feelings, desires, attractions and urges that you decide to say "No," to, is that **the next step is often experiencing grief**.

You have chosen to die to self, which is quite unpopular today, and that can leave you lonely.

What would motivate someone to give up something they want? Seeing a bigger picture and a greater reward. This is why our theology matters.

So, is attraction to the same sex sin? I do not think so.

Attraction is part of the data being processed that leads someone to make a decision.

Will this define me? Will I act on this feeling? What do I do? Who am I? Am I gay? What does God want from me?

This is why we need the space to process, feel, hurt, ask questions, and grieve.

Your beliefs about attractions ought to inform all your other relationships. Think about it this way: if I lined up five hundred men and five hundred women and had you decide who stays and who goes based on attraction, you could eliminate a lot of them easily from the line. If we took this a step further, and you had a lengthy conversation with each person, you could eliminate even more from the line, both male and female.

I would dare say that for many of us, in the first (and even second) evaluation we very well might eliminate the person that might be the best match for us in marriage, or the person that might be our future best friend. So, what am I saying?

Attraction is a bad measuring stick.

Beware of how much weight you place on feelings and attraction—no matter what stage of life you are in, single or married.

I could go into a lot of the biology behind attraction and same-sex attraction, but I don't believe that will be helpful for most parents. The purpose of this section is for you to learn some skills and gain some perspective to help your son or daughter navigate their attractions so that they live guided by an ETHOS that is not based on what they feel. This goes for us as parents as well.

WHAT DO I SAY OR DO?

Have you ever made an impulsive purchase without stopping to check your budget? What about realizing you have blanked out while driving and do not remember the past few miles and turns? These are examples of how easily we act without thinking. Are we thinking — yes, we are — our operating system is running in the background, in our subconscious. If it is so outside of our consciousness—our awareness—did we really think it through? Nope.

The goal is to move our decision making to the forefront, to the **prefrontal cortex**, so that there can be an honest evaluation and appraisal of the decision to be made. If you do this in front of your children, you are showing them, through your example, of the process that they need to go through when they need to make a wise decision.

Doing this as a couple when you make a decision on a big purchase "as a family" is an important lesson for your children to see.

Act impulsively as a parent and — surprise! — your children will most likely act impulsively as well.

Model moving things out of the subconscious into the decision making center — the **prefrontal cortex** — and you are giving your children a layer of defense against the part of themselves that wants to act based on their emotions and impulses, which cannot be trusted.

Sin loves the operating system of the subconscious. It can sit there and work in the background, corroding the system, and we don't even notice. We must be leaders. We must help expose sin and darkness. We need to do so in a tactful manner though, so that the future relationship is preserved.

So, what should you do if your son or daughter expresses they have attractions toward the same-sex?

Listen. Be patient. Challenge them to think deeper. Have conversations that are shaping of their worldview, but not demanding that they conform, or feel something they do not feel. **The more that these feelings and attractions can be processed verbally and not in the subconscious operating system, the better.** This could be with you, a caring Christian counselor, a mentor, or a teacher.

Do these feelings ever change? Actually, yes, they do.

This is why we must be vigilant earlier than we probably expect in order to have these defining and honest *micro-conversations* regarding what is right and wrong. You can do this intentionally, or society and the media will be glad to do it for you.

Remember the space of same sex attraction that I was talking about earlier? This is what I want you to be able to create. Once an identity is settled upon, and once they have engaged in sexual activity with the same sex, further movement becomes much more difficult. The process of identity formation is a critical process we all go through. It matters who we say we are and how we define ourselves. This goes for all areas and parts of ourselves.

If you tell yourself that you're just a lazy bum, don't be surprised at how this plays out down the road.

If you tell yourself you are not smart and that you can't learn, you'll find your limiting beliefs are becoming true in your life. **So, take every thought captive.** Scrutinize it, and decide whether it is capital "T" Truth or not. Do this consciously, intentionally, and knowing that it will be a battle. Do not settle for being guided by feelings or attractions. Don't let a desire become your identity.

CARE AND COMPASSION — A BIBLICAL RESPONSE

Moms and dads often ask me how they can love their child without accepting or supporting their behavior or lifestyle. This is a heart wrenching place to be in as a leader or parent.

There is a setup in the system today that allows only two options going forward.

You must either accept me as I am, without asking anything of me;

or, you hate me.

It is scary and limiting to view reality this way. So many people, young and old, make a decision that changes their life forever and has a huge impact on those that love them, yet everyone else must remain silent and accept it or be labeled a hater.

What you and your child believe about love matters. Some people's definition of love means that others cannot use their own discernment, make judgments, or question anything they do. This person will seldom see growth or maturity.

Other people have a definition of love that allows others to use their own discernment, challenge them, and disagree. This person will experience growth and enjoy their relationships.

Which of these is biblical? I would have to say the latter one. **God loves us so much that He does NOT let us stay as we are, but expects growth, maturity, and sacrifice so that we become more and more like Christ every day.** The first definition of love demands its own way and is looking out only for itself — not the other person.

So, what does care and compassion look like? It is being gentle, yet still pushing. It is having compassion, but not lowering your standards.

When you were five years old, the bar was pretty low. At fifteen, it goes higher. At twenty-five it rises again. When you were a new believer, you were adopted with NO requirements. Ten years later though, you were being shaped, challenged, and there was an expectation that your life would bear fruit.

Expect more out of others. Expect more out of them, though, with care and compassion — not an iron fist or with demands.

Think of it this way: **You are playing the long game.** They may not be willing to listen to you today, so remain in their life, listen, be compassionate, show genuine care for them.

Playing the long game is staying "in relationship" so that when their life falls apart — and it does in everyone's story — you are there and have been there as a constant reminder of God's love.

Remember that loving another is **ALL** about the long game. God is at work. You are only a small instrument. He changes people. Nagging, sarcasm, and anger are not tools He uses.

Be consistent in your love for them. Wait expectantly for an opening to enter a new level of relationship where they may listen to you for the first time. Be present, even if it is uncomfortable. Choose your battles wisely, ruled by God's love for them, and with care and compassion. What is this compassion?

It is a breaking heart for someone you deeply love. It is patience. It is endurance. It is the long game.

CHAPTER 6

WHAT MY CHILD IS FACING TODAY

As a parent, it is often overwhelming to think about how much the world has changed since we were children and all the things our children will face that we did not even know existed when we were younger. The truth of the matter is that our children are a target. If an advertiser can hook them when they are young, then they will have a customer for life. This is true for all products — from phone and computer apps to pornography and the food industry. Some industries sell products and services that are morally and ethically neutral. Others are predators, preying on our kid's naiveté and their unquenchable curiosity.

Pornography is a powerful force that has entered nearly every life and home in some form or fashion. There is no place for it in a biblical sexual ethic. It steals. It distorts. It harms relationships and destroys families. It rewires the brain.

Mark 7:20–23 reminds us of the person we are dealing with both in ourselves and our children:

"And then he added, 'It is what comes from inside that defiles you. For from within, out of a person's heart, come evil thoughts, sexual immorality, theft, murder, adultery, greed, wickedness, deceit, lustful desires, envy, slander, pride, and foolishness. All these vile things come from within; they are what defile you'" (NLT).

These desires and our bent toward these things is normal, but is that truly what we want — normal? Broken? Or do we want a grander story for our children and ourselves?

Pornography

Sara, aged ten, slams the computer closed as her mom enters the room. She runs off. Her mother opens the laptop and the browser to find pictures of naked people. What should she do? Her next move matters tremendously.

Jeff easily found a way around his parents' internet filters and goes to his drug of choice multiple times a day. He is only thirteen years old and has spent hours on devices that his parents didn't know could access pornography. He doesn't own a cell phone, laptop, or tablet. He uses his iPod touch, his old Gameboy, and the browser in his video game system. He knows how to hide his tracks and his parents have no idea of his secret life.

Pam is eleven and has discovered that she gets a good feeling when she looks at videos on her smartphone. Her parents gave her the phone to keep her safe since she walks home from school alone every day. She spends hours each day watching pornography and scrolling through images from the time she arrives home from school until her parents return home from work.

The reality is that pornography is nearly inescapable.

I have often wondered who will show it to my kids first. Someone will. I promise.

Let me sum up everything that needs to be said here in one sentence:

YOU as the PARENT must have *micro-conversations* with your children, while they are young, about what is and is not okay regarding nudity, images, and video.

YOU are the one! If you don't prepare them ahead of time, someone will be able to win them over quite easily. It only takes one viewing to be sucked in. Even though most children report that their first time viewing pornography elicited a "gross" response, it pulls at their natural curiosity and draws them back in for more.

How can we limit the attraction and draw of this powerful drug?

TALK ABOUT IT! Be honest regarding its impact on YOUR heart and relationships. Explain that it distorts love, intimacy, and peace. Talk about your own struggles when they are mature enough to handle it. I know that can be tricky. Be honest. Be real. Be candid.

Pornography rewires the brain for **novelty**. It makes the ability to settle down with one spouse and find satisfaction nearly impossible. Today's pornography is more shocking, abusive, and disturbing than ever before. It lacks true intimacy, yet the viewer is drawn in by the skin, bodies, and freedom that many wish for.

True freedom in sex is not what we see in pornography. Pornography is bondage. It is never enough. Sex has become a drug and it NEVER truly satisfies. No one person will ever be enough. As screens have become a larger part of our lifestyle, virtual reality has become a new form of pornography. No human being can measure up to an avatar.

Marriages fail. True intimacy loses.

Many of the women that film porn videos view this work as a step up from where they were before and my heart breaks for them. Doing porn, dancing naked on stage for money, prostituting and offering escorting services are places where many of them find value, respect, and even worship. They may love the attention and power, yet they are still being exploited. We cannot deny that part either. Many remain in this line of work because it gives them a sense of satisfaction and a sense of control. This ought to be eye-opening.

Nudity has a place and a context biblically. It is reserved for marriage between one man and one woman. Outside of that protective relationship, nudity decreases in value, is cheapened, and erodes. Ironically, our culture sees this as freedom. It isn't though. It is bondage.

Freedom is not having to worry about sexually transmitted infections and diseases.

Freedom is giving and receiving love that honors and serves, gives, and respects.

Freedom is sexual satisfaction and enjoyment without pressure, demand, exchange of money, or performance. Ironically, freedom is found in marriage. Monogamy.

The only place that naturally creates life is the sexual relationship between a man and a woman. Sex is more than a game for fun, for self, for pleasure, or for release. It must always and forever remain in the context and protection of a relationship. Let us raise the bar to require just that — relationship. Commitment. Boundaries.

What should Sara's mom do now, after catching her ten-year-old viewing explicit content online?

This is the time for a ***micro-conversation***. This is NOT the time for a lecture. This is NOT the time to yell at her and make her feel shame. The truth is that Sara probably already feels shame inside even though she does not know how to express it. Your job is to help her process what she has seen. We want her to let go of the shame trapped inside her young body and be free. Shame takes deeper root and sets its talons in her heart and soul the longer she holds it inside. Comfort her. Help her have a safe space to process, feel, and ask questions — even explicit ones. The truth is that whatever "innocence" she had before, it is gone now. Treat her with care, but also as if she is a bit older than she may be. She is now stewarding a heavier load in her head and heart.

Help her carry it. How? You can help by moving her thoughts and habits out of the subconscious into the prefrontal cortex.

Help her evaluate it.

Help her decide out loud what is best and what is harmful. This is not something you can do for her, but you can walk her toward a decision and let her make it. You are the guide, while your child is the main character. Be a great guide.

NUDITY YESTERDAY AND TODAY

For many of our children, the first time they view pornography they do not see a naked picture like many of us did. They are viewing videos of gross and abusive scenes that most of us would consider horrifying.

Think about this: If this is their first exposure, where do they go from there? Honestly, today, it has gone to places most of us cannot imagine. If you go online and search for any cartoon your kids love and add the word porn to it, you will find that someone has taken those animated characters and turned them into sexual fiends. One I recently learned about is My Little Pony porn. Each pony has huge breasts **and** a penis. Think about that. This is not normal and quite confusing. Another new form of pornography today is men who have undergone hormone replacement to grow breasts, and now possess both sexes' sexual parts. These men are shown engaging in sexual play with other men like them. Think about the implications of this on an eight- to thirteen-year-old son or daughter. It is confusing and seriously damaging to their future relationships and sexual ethic.

Knowing that nudity and sexual activity to the perverse extremes that are available online, just a few clicks away, on a device we can carry in our pockets, is downright terrifying. With all that is out there, it is tempting to say that it isn't a big deal if our kids happen to see a naked picture of a man or woman as God created them. However, Scripture states there should not be
    "even a hint of sexual immorality" (Ephesians 5:3, NIV).

The impact of sexual images on our hearts and minds is immeasurable. Of all things, graphic videos portraying sex between multiple people is nothing short of abusive and animalistic. This is an unacceptable image. **Sex is about relationship.** This is God's design for sexual intimacy — to be reserved and preserved for the marriage relationship with one man and one woman. There is NO other place.

The nudity of past years in magazine spreads, calendars, and posters had a huge impact on society, drawing men and women into a space they never should have gone. Most of you reading this can attest to how naked pictures impacted you when you were young. This is nothing though when compared to what many of our children are watching or will see in their first exposure of pornography today.

Imagine the impact that these easily accessible video clips with abuse and "anything goes" will have on our children.

Imagine the even graver impact it will have on our children if they see these things and never have a place to verbally process what they have seen. We have a chance if we can move it from the subconscious to the conscious — to the prefrontal cortex. How do we do this? **By asking hard questions, being willing to listen, suspending judgment, and teaching and leading patiently.** This is a dark subject with a tremendous impact on our sons' and daughters' future lives.

INTIMACY CHALLENGED AND REDEFINED

Consider the impact of these video clips on a viewer's understanding and framework for what is healthy between a man and woman in marriage. This assumes that a biblical sexual ethic is vocally being taught in your home. This is not successfully accomplished with lectures and the degrading of others' choices, but through *micro-conversations* over time that lead to your son or daughter making up their mind to choose God's design for marriage and intimacy.

Imagine how their intimacy will be affected after a few years of viewing pornography.

Imagine the impact that the constant download of video clips into their brains over the course of years will have on them if they decide to marry.

How will pornography influence their view of how they should treat their "love" and/or how they should be treated? This is HUGE!

This is why it is SO important that we become the small voice in our children's developmental years to create a healthy framework for marriage and intimacy. They need to be able to recognize healthy touch so that they can discern abuse in all its forms. **This requires that we be willing to "go there" and have thought through our own beliefs on the subject.**

Is the use of pornography okay in marriage as a marriage aid? Is it okay to use sexual toys, dildos, props, sexy lingerie? Is it okay to engage in anal sex or mutual masturbation? Is it okay to "swing" with other couples? Where are the lines? Does the Bible have anything to say on this subject?

It is important to know where you stand on these issues so that you can have *micro-conversations* that guide your growing children. The Lord entrusted them to you so that you can raise them up
"in the way they should go" (Proverbs 22:6 NKJV).

SEX OVER RELATIONSHIP

A final aspect to consider is where pornography puts sex in comparison to relationship. Sex trumps relationship. Relationships require time, patience, managing differences, having conversations, and compromise. Sex requires almost nothing. A lonely future awaits our children if they buy into the belief that sex is "no big deal." If you have ever watched video clips of porn or XXX movies, then you know that there is always something important missing in each encounter, despite the drama and cinematic wizardry. It is all "doing" and completely void of intimacy and relationship. This is a million miles away from God's design. It is not about the bigger orgasm, longer foreplay, or the experience of ecstasy. Sex was meant to bring together a husband and wife to do three things — yes three things — provide pleasure, protection, and procreation.

Scripture is clear about our hearts, our minds, our eyes, and our bodies. Here are a few samples:

Job 31:1

"I made a covenant with my eyes not to look with lust at a young woman" (NLT).

Proverbs 5:18–20

"Let your wife be a fountain of blessing for you. Rejoice in the wife of your youth. She is a loving deer, a graceful doe. Let her breasts satisfy you always. May you always be captivated by her love. Why be captivated, my son, by an immoral woman, or fondle the breasts of a promiscuous woman?" (NLT).

Proverbs 6:32

"But the man who commits adultery is an utter fool, for he destroys himself" (NLT).

Matthew 5:27–28

"You have heard the commandment that says, 'You must not commit adultery.' But I say, anyone who even looks at a woman with lust has already committed adultery with her in his heart'" (NLT).

Matthew 6:22–23

"Your eye is like a lamp that provides light for your body. When your eye is healthy, your whole body is filled with light. But when your eye is unhealthy, your whole body is filled with darkness. And if the light you think you have is actually darkness, how deep that darkness is!" (NLT).

Romans 13:13–14

"Because we belong to the day, we must live decent lives for all to see. Don't participate in the darkness of wild parties and drunkenness, or in sexual promiscuity and immoral living, or in quarreling and jealousy. Instead, clothe yourself with the presence of the Lord Jesus Christ. And don't let yourself think about ways to indulge your evil desires" (NLT).

1 Corinthians 6:18–20

"Run from sexual sin! No other sin so clearly affects the body as this one does. For sexual immorality is a sin against your own body. Don't you realize that your body is the temple of the Holy Spirit, who lives in you and was given to you by God? You do not belong to yourself, for God bought you with a high price. So you must honor God with your body" (NLT).

Colossians 3:5

"So put to death the sinful, earthly things lurking within you. Have nothing to do with sexual immorality, impurity, lust, and evil desires. Don't be greedy, for a greedy person is an idolater, worshiping the things of this world" (NLT).

1 Thessalonians 4:3–8

"God's will is for you to be holy, so stay away from all sexual sin. Then each of you will control his own body and live in holiness and honor—not in lustful passion like the pagans who do not know God and his ways. Never harm or cheat a fellow believer in this matter by violating his wife, for the Lord avenges all such sins, as we have solemnly warned you before. God has called us to live holy lives, not impure lives. Therefore, anyone who refuses to live by these rules is not disobeying human teaching but is rejecting God, who gives his Holy Spirit to you" (NLT).

Hebrews 13:4

"Give honor to marriage, and remain faithful to one another in marriage. God will surely judge people who are immoral and those who commit adultery" (NLT).

Bullying

Is your son or daughter a bully or being bullied?
Were you bullied as a kid, or were you a bully?

I know that these are not the only two options, but it seems like the case.

A better question to ask of ourselves is whether our son or daughter is a leader or a follower.

A follow-up question is, if they are a leader, where are they leading others — toward good or evil?

If they are a follower, are they discerning as to who they follow and what they will do? No one wants to see their child bullied and most of us hope that our child will not resort to bullying, which is an indicator of weakness and immaturity. Instead, we want to teach them to be discerning in who they follow and in how they lead others.

We should attempt to inspire our children to be defenders of the weak and voiceless, so that they will stand up for what is right, speak out against evil, and be change agents for good. Based on how our children manage social media, smartphones, and entertainment, we have a clue as to how they will handle this responsibility.

A key role we play as parents is in how we treat other people in our lives.

How do you respond when a coach doesn't treat your child the way you think they should?

Do you become belligerent and aggressive?

Do you speak critically of other children, adults, or teachers in your child's life, which they pick up on and then mimic your disrespectful tone and stance?

Could they pick up on your prejudice toward minorities and act on that?

Parents need to engage with their children on these topics before they become an issue. It may seem like you do not need to have this conversation, but many parents are shocked to find that the behavior of their children away from home or online is quite different from what they portray to their parents.

Do not let yourself believe that your son or daughter would never bully someone else and so never speak to them about it.

Don't assume that your child isn't being bullied because they don't tell you. Be the initiator of *micro-conversations* that take place day after day, week after week, so that your beliefs have weight with them and they know they can trust you.

SOCIAL MEDIA

Today, most of us use social media in some way. Many people, though, do NOT use this tool appropriately. It is a venue for posting lies, comparing experiences, and feeling jealousy and hatred toward themselves and others.

Social media etiquette and ethics must be taught prior to our children having access. There should be *micro-conversations* about what one ought to post, and what is questionable. They need to be taught to distinguish between what is true and what might be a lie. They need to know that it can be misused, abused, and part of illegal activity.

Many teenagers and parents do not realize that naked pictures of yourself when you are under the age of eighteen is child pornography. Period!

Both the sender and the recipient may be liable for having these pictures on their device. It is critical that our children know this beforehand so that they do not have to deal with the consequences after the fact.

It is imperative that you impress upon your children in your day-to-day conversations that anything posted online or sent via email or text, is public and can come back to haunt them in the future.

The truth of the matter is that too many kids have killed themselves over what others have posted about them in a public forum or sent to them privately via social media. Social media has become another venue that a bully uses to harass your child. Teach them while they are young to think about the persona they are portraying online in ALL they do.

Teach them to be alert for others that are being bullied and to be the young man or woman that stands up for those being harmed. **Teach them to use social media as a convenient tool to communicate and to connect with friends.**

It can even serve as an extension of a face to face community where friends can share funny things. Keep it light. Help them learn to be careful about what they share — both in personal matters and about hot topics. A lot of false information is available online, and if they are going to be part of that world, they need to be wise to its ways.

SMARTPHONES

Most adults and increasing numbers of teens and children have smartphones. **I wonder if parents realize the power of the device they are entrusting to their kids.** The computer behind the smartphone is more powerful than ALL the computers used in 1969 to get us to the moon. Isn't that mind boggling?

So, what are we entrusting them with besides a $500–$1000 device? We are giving our children access to everything — to the world.

I call them "porn portals."

On a smartphone, you can open Safari, click on Google, type in "porn" or "boobs" or "sex," click again, and you will find text-based results. At the top of the screen are two additional choices that, if chosen, will alter your child's life forever. The choices: "images" and "videos."
Do you truly realize the implications of what our children are carrying in their pockets?

I will be the first to say that this is NOT about keeping them from everything — and I say this as a homeschool dad! This is ALL about teaching them, training them, and permitting them to steward some choices for themselves. The earlier they are taught to do this, the greater the chance they will have a strong ETHOS as they enter adulthood.

I have seen too many families that shelter their children and are then surprised when their child is getting around filters, seeking out videos and images they shouldn't see, and deliberately disobeying family rules. Many have not been allowed to steward small things and now that they are older and MUST be prepared to steward greater things, they are ill-prepared. The key to preparing them rests again with hundreds of *micro-conversations* over the course of time.

Smartphones are not bad — they allow us to track our kids and keep in touch with them throughout the day. They allow our kids to stay connected with friends and call us if they are in need or danger. They can give a child a sense of security.

They are great for taking pictures and sharing memories with friends. They are not evil — they are a tool. Alcohol is not evil either, but if they are not stewarded well, both smartphones and alcohol are dangerous.

Who is talking to your kids about smartphones the most — you, or their friends and advertisers? Let it be you!

T.V. AND MOVIES

Stewardship is also critical when it comes to T.V. and movies because of the overwhelming choices that kids have access to. A lack of access leads many kids to seek out media elsewhere in ways that are more harmful. As you can tell, parents have a difficult task of maintaining the tension between free rein and lockdown. To do so, you must set a good example.

First, are you managing this for yourself in a way that you can confidently say, "Watch me?"

Secondly, what sort of *micro-conversations* are you having about what they have already viewed?

I took my kids to see a movie recently that had a few scenes that were subtly sexual. I talked separately with each of my kids about those scenes. I was surprised by what they noticed.

My twelve-year-old son noticed the sexual and was uncomfortable.

My ten-year-old son just laughed and focused on the guy that was hit in the crotch — he is such a goofball!

My eight-year-old daughter thought the girl's dress was beautiful.

What did your kids think about that scene in the latest movie or TV show you watched as a family?

I don't know, I wasn't there. They were thinking something though! Ask them. Let them tell you. Create a safe space to have those *micro-conversations*. Use specific scenes to highlight conversations about how someone was treated, about modesty, strength, power, friendship, and sacrifice. Use scenes to create dialogues about who they hope to be when they grow up, or what they would do if they were in that situation.

The more intentional you are about having these *micro-conversations* as you are viewing various shows / movies, the more your child's ETHOS will be crafted intentionally to look like yours. Be assertive. Be ahead of the game. Start when they are young. Any cartoon or commercial can be used as a teaching moment and an opportunity for another *micro-conversation.*

Influence And Idols

As you know others outside the family can be powerful influences on our children, especially as they enter the teen years. They care more and more about what others think. They look up to others more than they used to and tend to think less of their parents, but this does not have to be the case. Children tend to grab onto a role model as they are beginning to think more seriously about what they want to do in the future. Some will feel pressure to stand out while others hope to go by unnoticed. The comparison factor can become scary. Looks. Talent. Status. Position. Clothing. Devices. This is the reality our children live with at school, youth group, and playing on sports teams, bands, and almost anywhere else you can imagine. It is truly inescapable.

So, what can we do as parents to be proactive, intentional, and ahead of the curve?

My advice continues to come down to our *microconversations* on these subjects as we acknowledge the pressures they are facing on a daily basis. We can turn it around and challenge them to think about who they want to look up to.

From my observation of families over the past nineteen years as a family counselor, there is little intentionality in truly discipling our children — shaping our children to live and love and be more like Christ.

Instead, there is an emphasis on academic and/or athletic success, on sports and fun and games, on keeping them entertained, — or there is neglect. Your children are watching you. They will lean toward embracing your heroes, or rejecting them, with almost no middle ground, depending on whether they deem that you are sane or not. I know this seems crazy and even funny, but they can easily become mini versions of you. They can also, just as easily, reject everything we stand for as parents and as a family. It is their choice.

Key areas that I see influencing this outcome are how we handle "stars," whether we have a healthy community, intentionally modeling saying "no" and living with boundaries, especially when those boundaries are unpopular.

STARS AND IDOLS

The way that we relate to celebrities impacts our children. Each parent should be intentional about what they invest their time and effort in what they watch, and — if we are not careful — who we worship. The culture that we create at home is all they know at first. Are you a groupie to someone?

How do you talk about celebrities, sports heroes, singers, and politicians?

When does admiring someone for their skill or talent move into idolatry?

A key indicator is if we begin choosing games, concerts, and screen time OVER real face to face interactions.

I grew up in Chile, South America, and when my family moved back to the United States I observed an obsession with sports in the United States that has always felt strange to me. It took me years to be able to see any good in sports at all, since I saw it negatively impacting so many friends and families.

I finally saw that there was a crucial difference between some families. There are those that worship a team or a sport and it keeps them from deep, real relationships. And there are families that use sports to further relationships with others by laughing, playing, relaxing, and enjoying time with friends. This is the critical line.

How does your relationship with the stars impact your children and family — both in time and in money?

How do these impact other relationships when looking at the kind of example you are passing on to your children?

A LACK OF COMMUNITY

Why does this matter? Too many of us lack community. Galatians 6:2 reminds us that we must:
"Share each other's burdens, and in this way obey the law of Christ" (NLT).

I believe that most of us — especially men — do not know what this would even look like. We attend church and we go to various events, but we are truly friendless.

Who are the other adults speaking into your life and into your kids' lives?

Men — dads — do you have a band of brothers? I don't mean a group of buddies you spend time with to the neglect of your family. I mean men you look up to and that you could call on, day or night, if you were in need.

Ladies — moms — do you have relationships that encourage you, lift you up, and are women you could call on if you were in need?

When I speak of community I am thinking of those people whom you invest in, and they in turn invest in you. You should carefully evaluate the communities that both you and your children are invested in. An influential teacher or coach can lead a child in a direction opposite that which you would choose for them, or they can come alongside you and be a voice your child listens to when they don't want to listen to mom or dad.

Which people or groups do you spend the majority of your time with?

Some participate in various sports teams, school committees or clubs. Others are involved in church events or civic groups.

Have you thought intentionally through the impact of those relationships on who YOU are, not to mention the impact on your kids and family?

How can you expand or limit (as needed) those influencing you, your kids, and your family?

What needs to change?

Is there anyone that you should be careful to limit spending time with because they drag you down and their cynicism weighs on your soul?

Is there anyone that you should invest more time with because they are an encouragement and true friend?

Now let's flip that around — do you bring people down when they're around you?

Or are you a source of joy, encouragement, and challenge to your friends?

Be extremely intentional with your community. I have seen families and friends choose a community due to the interests of their children that in turn destroyed their family. These activities can end up pulling a family in too many directions and cause harm.

The fact is that today's average family is overworked and overly stressed. Choose how you spend your time wisely. Be attentive that you don't push your children in a direction you think is best, but that leads them to resent you and the direction you chose for them. Also, be careful you do not cater to your child's every whim. Time is not an unlimited resource and it is good for our children to see us prioritize our time, giving preference to those things that build up our family and our faith.

Proverbs 18:24 says:
"There are 'friends' who destroy each other, but a real friend sticks closer than a brother" (NLT). Be that second kind of friend to others, modeling for your children in all you do.

Proverbs 17:17 says:
"A friend is always loyal, and a brother is born to help in time of need" (NLT).

John 15:13 says:
"There is no greater love than to lay down one's life for one's friends" (NLT).

REASONS TO SAY "NO" AND LIVE WITH BOUNDARIES

A difficult, but crucial aspect of raising children is understanding that boundaries are good, necessary, and an expression of love. Most children (and some parents!) believe boundaries are unloving and uncaring.

Can you say "NO" to things, or do you struggle with overcommitting? This impacts you, your family, and your children's view of work, church, and others in need.

There are so many needs right in front of us, and it seems impossible to say "NO" to anything. We can be encouraged by Jesus's example here. Jesus, in His few years of ministry, exemplified boundaries. He took time away from the crowds and spent time in prayer with His Father. He invested heavily into His disciples — His closest friends.

Do we do this?

Or do we live and act as if we are above this kind of need? Yikes!

If Jesus needed them, how much more do we? We need game nights and barbeques with friends, but we also need quiet evenings with just our family. We need to spend time in ministry — and time in a hammock. We must take care of ourselves and our family.

The amount of sleep you get each night matters and impacts everyone around you. Your body also uses this time to heal and file memories away into your long-term memory.

Your time with God matters.

Your time with family and friends matters.

Rest is rejuvenating. Somehow, these times that are life altering have been demoted.

I believe that a contributing factor to the increase in mental and physical health issues is a lack of boundaries. Why do I say boundaries?

In order to eat well, you must take the time to prepare a healthy meal. You can't pick up fast food on the way to ball practice every evening and expect to be healthy. You must carve out space — a boundary — into your schedule that allows you to take care of the health needs of those you love. **In order to find rest and rejuvenation you must set aside time and protect it in your schedule.**

I heard once of a leader that had a business meeting scheduled on his calendar daily from 5–6pm. When someone was trying to schedule a meeting with him, they were frustrated that he would not consider moving this appointment and asked him what was so important. His reply was, "Dinner with my family. When I put 'dinner with family' on the calendar, it kept getting shuffled and seen as a lesser priority. This way I keep it protected." What a great example. Are you setting up boundaries?

Boundaries encourage and invite freedom!

They create an ecosystem of health and wellness in relationships and spiritual renewal.

Philippians 3:5–6 describes how Paul was "all in" committed to his interpretation of the law. This led him to persecute Christians and to live his version of perfection. Verses 7–9 show the shift in priorities:

> "I once thought these things were valuable, but now I consider them worthless because of what Christ has done. Yes, everything else is worthless when compared with the infinite value of knowing Christ Jesus my Lord. For his sake, I have discarded everything else, counting it all as garbage, so that I could gain Christ and become one with him. I no longer count on my own righteousness through obeying the law; rather I become righteous through faith in Christ" (NLT).

We live for Him. Let's help our children choose to do the same.

CHAPTER 7

RAISING SEXUALLY HEALTHY CHILDREN

I am hoping that at this point your heart, passion, and desire is to lead your family with confidence and intentionality toward a biblical sexual ethic. There are many other aspects of our lives that matter as well, but they are beyond the scope of this book. **Raising sexually healthy children requires commitment to a specific ETHOS.** It then requires that we, as parents, learn how to pass that on in bite sized *micro-conversations* as our children grow and receive information from the world around them.

A key piece of the puzzle — for you and for your children — will be found in how you manage hurts, failures, and disappointments. Too many parents and their children are trapped in shame loops that are generational.

Break the cycle. Find freedom. Find joy. Then, once you have found it, pass it on.

Imagine looking at your grown children and seeing that they have made thoughtful, informed decisions that they can defend rather than emotional and impulsive ones. Imagine being proud of the young man or woman they have become. Imagine a sense of gratitude for the adults God entrusted to you who have made the decision to be godly change agents in the world.

It Starts With You ~ The Parent

Jared and **Kendra** knew that they both had rough lives growing up and they wanted something different for their children. With the birth of their first son, they began teaching him about his body, about sexuality, dating, and marriage. They continued this with each of their children as five more siblings were added to the family. They invited hard (and weird!) questions from their children and answered them the best they could. As a result of their honesty about their own failings, their stories of childhood abuse, and the role God played in their story, their six children avoided much of the pain and heartache that many unnecessarily face today. Their children did not all arrive at adulthood without drama or failures, but none of them had the excuse of ignorance or naiveté. As each of them walked through their adolescent years, they encountered struggles with pornography and dating when they were too young due to peer pressure. They knew though, without any doubt, what their parents believed, what their parents' expectations were for them, and that they were responsible for their own actions before God.

All six of Jared and Kendra's children eventually married and they were joyous occasions. All six of them remain faithful in their pursuit of God in their adult lives, passing the same down to their own children. Even though they didn't have one hundred percent success in all of their choices, they each knew their parents loved them. They knew that God loved them enough to die for them. And they knew that they could choose. Through the knowledge given to them by their parents, they were better positioned to make their choices. They could clearly see the destination each choice could potentially lead to and they could "choose" with wisdom. What a beautiful picture.

Do you want that?

This begins with your one-year-old, your two-year-old, your three-year-old, and so on. Start today, if you have not already. Begin by intentionally helping each of your children craft their own biblical sexual ethic — their ETHOS.

Use short, meaningful conversations — *micro-conversations* — to plant seeds, and as you intentionally water them you will see them grow before your eyes.

HELPING YOUR CHILDREN DEVELOP THEIR ETHOS

So how do we pull all of this together for our children?

Jeff is a seventeen-year-old young man who has been trained to live by a biblical sexual ethic. His parents prepared him well.

He is respectful of authority.

He honors women and avoids areas of temptation.

He has struggled with pornography, but has chosen to die to those desires and fill his life with better things.

He has a great relationship with his parents and his siblings.

He has great relationships with girls his age and hasn't dated.

He has a healthy view of marriage, thanks to years of *micro-conversations.*

Recently, they have led to longer conversations about the reality of marriage, its struggles, and its joys. Jeff is eager to leave home, see the world, and have new adventures. He has decided on a degree from a college that will set him up to have an income that will allow him to support missionaries, invest in ministries that change the world, and support the family he hopes to have one day.

Jennifer is a twenty-one-year-old young woman living on her own. She is watching her friends get in and out of sexual relationships, mocking marriage, and spending money like there is no tomorrow while they mooch off their parents to pay for their cell phone bill, car insurance, and miscellaneous purchases.

She remembers all those uncomfortable conversations with her mom and dad that helped inform her about her body, her health, God's design for sex, marriage, parenting, and even friendships. She is very thankful that she can easily reject the world that her friends are asking her to join.

She wants a more peaceful life with less heartbreak, no scares of a sexually transmitted infection, no worries about pregnancy. She has financial stability and is willing to wait for a husband who will treat her with respect and as an equal partner in marriage.

These scenarios are possible due to daily and weekly investment into our children's ETHOS. Our intentional *micro-conversations* have planted the seeds and paved the way for a confident, resilient, young adult.

Will this always yield positive results? NO.

Your children have free will and can reject everything you have taught them. This is also why I propose viewing this as the long game. You must do your part, but ultimately you are entrusting them to God and to their own decisions, since they are ultimately not your responsibility anyway. That is hard for most of us to grasp, believe, and live out. We tend to blame ourselves for their every mistake, but strangely enough, at the same time avoid acknowledging how we have been a negative influence. Be honest with yourself in this process. Be honest with them. You both will be better people because of it.

SHORT, MEANINGFUL CONVERSATIONS: PLANTING SEEDS

These are what I have been calling *micro-conversations*. They are not lectures. Sometimes they are a dialogue and at other times just a few sentences to plant an idea or perspective into your child's heart and mind.

Remember that this is not about us waiting for them to ask a question and being able to respond. That is great and wonderful, if it happens, but is not normal behavior. The norm is to have zero conversations about these topics because children and teens will not bring them up on their own. So be abnormal and "go there." Be abnormal and initiate hard conversations.

Do not wait until your daughter has a boy over and asks if she can go up to her room to study and close the door. She should know long before that even happens that this is not acceptable.

Do not wait until your sixteen-year-old wants to go out on a date alone and get serious with someone. Establish parameters, guidelines and steps that they need to take beforehand. Make these times early, helpful, and often — staying ahead of these crossroads where most teenagers and their parents collide.

Stay ahead of this with *micro-conversations* that ultimately leave the decisions in their hands as they grow up, but leave your voice in their heads!

Colossians 3:23 is a stern reminder to:
"Work willingly at whatever you do, as though you were working for the Lord rather than for people" (NLT).

That is how we must see our work with our children — as for the Lord.

INTENTIONALLY WATERING THOSE SEEDS

As you go about your days, water the seeds you planted about pornography. Walk past the fifty-foot breast in the window of Victoria's Secret in the mall and discuss its appropriateness there, what they are advertising, and how it impacts women and men.

Use scenes in movies and T.V. shows to open dialogue that leads into further discussions. Use news stories to discuss perpetrators and victims. To discuss harm. To discuss shame. Use these to talk to your daughters about being aware of their surroundings and what she should do if she is ever in a similar circumstance. Consider acting it out in a mild manner, so that she automatically responds rather than freezing.

Use family drama and the pains their friends experience to teach your children compassion, patience, and care for another in a difficult situation. Include all ages of your children. Listen to differing perspectives.

Be willing to be challenged. Invite disagreement. Let them learn here with you, so they can leave your home confident, compassionate, and eager to be a positive force in the lives of others, without compromising the gospel, Scripture, or their faith.

Boundaries And Choices

A critical dimension of our sexuality and sexual development are boundaries and choices. If those aren't well established, we are at the mercy of our feelings, desires, and peer pressure. To live within boundaries requires us to step back, recognize the difference that results from living within these, and thankful for their protection. Ironically, it is these boundaries that give us freedom.

When I graduated from seminary and began my life as a Licensed Professional Counselor. I was a single twenty-five-year-old male in a female dominated field. Ninety-nine percent of my clients were women and most of my friends were female. I was terrified. I had an ETHOS drilled into me from my family and my training regarding the importance of boundaries. I also knew of a few cases where one accusation of wrongdoing had sunk a person's reputation and career. I set up incredibly strict boundaries. These were for my freedom. Within these boundaries, I had less to worry about. Later, I was working at a college and was told I needed to loosen my boundaries if I was going to work with college students. I was surprised. I was also quite confused by the suggestion and wondered if I should loosen up. I quickly realized though that I had more freedom by using these boundaries and I added more — like never eating alone with a woman who was not my wife.

Boundaries are entrenched into your ETHOS at an early age as we learn from our families and absorb their energy and culture. As we begin to play that out in our lives, we free ourselves, adopting some of the constraints put on us by our families and dispensing with others. We — and our children — have the freedom to choose. Our culture speaks out of both sides of its mouth. On one hand we are told to be free and choose for ourselves whatever we want. But, on the other hand, if someone chooses to act with reservation, wisdom or within a biblical sexual ethic, they are ridiculed as if they made the "wrong" choice. Find freedom in boundaries, your choices, and in saying, "NO."

HOW TO SAY "NO"

Learning to say, "NO," is a crucial skill. We are always saying, "NO." In effect, every time we say, "Yes," to something — we are, in turn, saying, "NO," to something else.

Teach your children to say, "NO."

Teach them to have the vocal and internal ability to stand up for themselves and have boundaries. Most of us are familiar with the concept of fight or flight. If we get into a sticky situation, we have a release of adrenaline and we are, in a sense, forced to expend that energy by fighting, or fleeing. However, there is another response — freezing — that has serious consequences since the energy built up by adrenaline and angst rarely gets resolved.

When men and women that have been abused or violated tell their story, they usually regret not having spoken up, fought, or run away. Instead, they froze. However, despite — or maybe because of — freezing, they survived. They made it through. Now many remain stuck because the energy that was built up needs a place to go. It needs to be released. From this experience, they quickly learned to remain small and silent. Their ability to say, "NO," diminishes.

EXAMPLE

Lisa and **Brett** have invested in their children with a vision for their children's future success. They started young, teaching and training their children in a biblical sexual ethic. As they went into each year of life with their children they also knew that part of the bargain was trusting God in the raising of their children. Hope in things unseen. We are not guaranteed tomorrow. Your faith must be in God and His work in the lives of you and your children.

Hope breeds a peace that passes all understanding. Hope expects great things as well.

Hope for the best things for each of your children.

I want you to be able to place the most important thing at the top of your goals in the raising of your children.

What is this most important goal?

Dr. George Barna speaks of this goal in his book *Revolutionary Parenting*.[44]

What is your primary goal? With the primary goal Dr. Barna's research found all the other priorities we may have for our children will work themselves out.

Hope for great things! Expect much!

Be intentional at preparing them well. May your children become adults that are **"Champions for Christ."** — this ought to be our top goal.

Managing Hurts, Failures And Disappointments

As parents, we can do everything we are supposed to do and bad things can still happen.

Paul is a twenty-two-year-old that was taught a biblical sexual ethic, but chose to take his own path. He decided he had to try everything out for himself. Learning the hard way is a reality for many people. We grieve their choices. We love them. We pursue them. But we must also remember that these are their choices.

Julianna is eighteen and a survivor. She grew up in a great home with a loving, single mom that talked with her early, used *micro-conversations* often, and built into her daughter a solid sense of identity, strength, and a passion to live by a biblical sexual ethic. Her ETHOS was unshakeable. That is, it was unshakeable until her first boyfriend. She met a young man in college, and they began dating. By the end of their first year together she was a different person. He seemed to be sweet and caring, and said and did all the right things. He slowly nibbled away at her soul though with demeaning comments that she was not quite good enough. He would criticize her appearance, weight, intelligence, and decisions. Eventually, she had no resolve left and when he pushed on her boundaries physically, she had no fight left in her. She surrendered to his desires without a fight or a care. She did not realize what had been happening until it was too late.

I have heard this story numerous times from young women. The behavior of these "men" is disgusting and heartbreaking. This is grooming, leading to rape, even though there was no fight and no one said, "NO."

Jill grew up with a dad that loved her and she was a strong confident twenty-five-year-old even though her mom had left them years ago. Her dad was proactive, engaging, funny, and raised his little girl the best he knew how. She had a strong biblical sexual ethic — an ETHOS — and was excelling in all areas of her life as a teenager. She went to a party though and had something to drink that had been tampered with. She woke up the next morning in a lot of pain and bleeding. She had been "roughed up," and was unaware of what had truly happened at the party the night before. Now, at age twenty-five, she has grown in strength and resolve to help other girls never find themselves in a situation like that. She has a passion and calling that, when combined with her story, has propelled her to make a difference in a unique way that only someone in her shoes could do.

FREEDOM FROM SHAME

Shame steals everything — life, joy, desire, and a future. For many of us, our default setting is to stay here — to let it take up residence and settle. My hope and desire for you as a parent is that you can find freedom from shame in your own personal story. I want you to be able to see that when shame enters the story, it is only there to steal, kill, and destroy. Sound familiar? The marvelous truth is that God is a redeemer. Rest in this. Believe this. Live this out. Face that shame. Recognize that it only sucks you into a spiral of self-hatred and hatred of others. Realize that it only steals your joy and any desire you might have left.

Dr. Dan Allender explains in his speaking and writing how shame can be overcome. The unlikely source of joy is found in being broken. To feel sorrow and grieve your loss allows you to then find yourself in a place of gratitude with no room for contempt or hatred. You can now dance for joy. What does this dance look like? This freedom? This joy?

It is being truly broken and then, as Proverbs 31:25 says: "She is clothed with strength and dignity; she can laugh at the days to come" (NIV).

What a beautiful picture of strength, grace, peace, and fearlessness that can laugh at the devil's schemes as you rest in God's perfect plan for your life.

So, what is the task for us?

First, we must address our story as parents.

What are you holding on to? Where are you all tied up by the enemy?

This can usually be found as you review your story.

I would dare say that we all have places in our story that need attention, care, and honesty.

FORGIVENESS

Paul had to try everything. He made his way. One of his biggest hurdles in finding freedom for himself will be forgiving himself for the pain he caused his family and others.

Julianna did nothing wrong. She knows that in her head, but doesn't feel it in her heart. She will need to forgive herself for trusting him, even though there was no way she could have known. She faces the insurmountable hurdle of forgiving her ex-boyfriend.

Jill beats herself up for going to that party and touching that drink. She has found forgiveness for the guys that raped her even in the vagueness of some of the memories.

Forgiveness is never saying it was okay. Forgiveness is loving someone in the way that God does — not giving them what they deserve for their actions or hearts. Truthfully, we all deserve one thing — and that is hell. By the grace of God, we are offered free, eternal life. Forgiveness is not something we do once we feel like it. It is a conscious choice of our own personal freedom. It is cutting the ties with someone that harmed us and still has a hold on us. This is so difficult for our emotions to grasp, which, if we are not careful, keep us captive.

Forgiveness is freedom. Be free!

GROWTH AND YOUR JOY

What comes from relieving ourselves of the burden of shame and resting in God's forgiveness?

We grow. We truly experience joy. We find freedom. We are who God created us to be — worshipers.

Let's look at this from another angle. Your son or daughter needs to learn about this process. They need to understand about the real world. They don't need us only for shelter. They need us to prepare them. They need us to prepare them for the hurts and disappointments that will inevitably come. They need us to teach them to stand up for themselves and for others. I was driving home from a movie recently with my oldest son and talking to him about the difficulty of going against the grain with friends — standing up for someone that is being picked on, or calling out dirty jokes and conversations that are disrespectful of women or others different from themselves as unacceptable. It starts with one. He can be that one.

Lead your children into parts of your story — your successes and your failures. This should be done carefully, taking into consideration their age, maturity, and discretion — meaning their understanding that some things that are shared within the family aren't to be shared publicly. They will learn more from your failures if you will be honest and real about how these affected you, hurt you, and even hurt others.

Face YOUR shame over past actions.

Face YOUR fears of being found out and being unloved.

Model for them how to live FREE.

Share YOUR story.

Enable them to speak up, to say, "NO," to flee when necessary, and to change the world around them.

You are the most influential person in their life from birth to about age ten. Around the age of eleven, everything changes. Remember, the teenage years do not have to be the nightmare that so many parents have with their children. They need to take more risks. **They MUST learn how to fail gracefully.** Let them learn this while they are under your watch so that you can show them how to get back up and try again.

This is a beautiful part of our calling as parents that began on the day of conception.

Prepare them to fail. Show them how to get back up.

Prepare them to face disappointment with a faith in God that brings them back to life, but know that this doesn't always happen overnight.

Prepare them to face heartache with a trust in their God that He even has all those details worked out for their good. He is a gracious God.

Rest in that as a parent.

Pass that peace that passes all understanding on to your children early (Philippians 4:7, NKJV) — the earlier the better.

CHAPTER 8

DATING, THE "M" WORD, AND TRAUMA

"Single, never married" is a status on the rise. "Newly single" (divorced) has also increased in past years. Whether they delay marriage or experience divorce, there is a high probability that your son or daughter will find themselves single as adults. They are still sexual beings though and need to develop the skills that will allow them to build healthy relationships and steward their sexuality.

Think through the following and commit to further study.

Do you have an approach, method, or system for healthy dating and relationship building that you can share with your child?

Do you want your child to do as you did? Building a strong, healthy framework for dating is critical in being able to avoid the pain that most seem to go through as young adults or when they find themselves single again after a marriage ends.

An arena of tremendous controversy in human sexuality is masturbation — the "M" word.

What does the medical field say?

What does culture say?

What about the Church?

What ought my response be to my son or daughter that engages in this behavior?

How do I teach them and prepare them to make wise, conscious choices?

As we learn more about trauma, the counseling community is realizing that its presence has a serious impact on the one who bears it. **It is critical to address past trauma as it tends to have a high rate of resurrection, haunting its victims.**

One of its tools that haunts and takes root is **shame**. Shame is a destroyer of our soul, our motivation, and any vision we might have had for a bright future. It cripples us in many areas of our life, robbing us of confidence and forward momentum.

Forgiveness, for many, is a "four-letter word," yet it holds the key to the freedom we desire. To be able to move beyond trauma, you and your child will need to be able to express both sorrow and gratitude.

Have you wept for the loss you endured due to the trauma?

Have you been able to orient your heart toward gratitude for the other blessings in your life?

Gratitude cannot co-exist with shame. The peace found in joy is not found through penance. Equipping our children with skills that will minimize the impact of potentially traumatic life events is a start. Developing resilience that helps them rise above difficulties, disappointments, and pain is a critical life skill. Yes, it will start with us learning the skills, but then we must intentionally lead our children in practical ways to manage their hurts. I want you to find this freedom to live and lead well. Keep reading.

Singleness, Sexuality, And Dating

Imagine that your son is sixteen and dating a fellow sixteen-year-old peer.

Are you ready?

Are they prepared to steward that kind of responsibility?

Your twenty-one-year-old is sexually active.

Are they prepared to steward that responsibility?

What is dating?

What is this word from the past called courtship?

I want to share a practical framework as you guide your children toward a biblical sexual ethic in their relationships with others.

SEXUALITY AND THE SINGLE ADULT

Your sons and daughters are sexual beings. They have been from birth. As they grow, the level of stewardship required is proportional to their physical and hormonal maturity. It does not come with a switch. It takes conscious decision making and forethought. Most of the decisions that I see teenagers and young adults making are based on convenience and impulse. **Let's develop forethought and strength of character in our children before they face the temptation of desire in their relationships.**

Your twelve-year-old needs guidance on how to steward these awkward feelings and attractions.

Are you teaching them or are you relegating this to their school or your church?

Imagine that your sixteen-year-old daughter has been invited to the prom by a senior. What your daughter does with this invitation and at this event will be determined by the hundreds of *micro-conversations* she has had with you over the years. These **micro-conversations** prepared her to have a plan and the confidence to execute that plan. I am not offering an opinion on whether she should go or not. That is up to you and the convictions of your family. I am saying that if she does choose to accept the invitation, it is imperative that she already have a biblical sexual ethic that guides her boundaries and that she can express and defend without apology.

Can you teach your child ethics and morals in their teen years and expect that to guide them to make wise decisions throughout their adolescence and young adult years?

This must have begun years earlier. Younger than you probably think. Help your child see that they are the stewards of their body and their attractions, desires, and leanings. They are the one responsible for their actions to others and to the Lord. Their actual thoughts and feelings are data points, but the next step of the choosing — action taking — is fully within their control. This is taught. This is modeled.

Celibate single adults face an uphill battle today. It requires an extremely honest assessment of God's Word and the risks and consequences of your choices. We choose. Our children choose. Part of our job in raising our children is to prepare them for the feelings, desires, and lusts that will pull at them from all directions. If you watch a car commercial for a car that is out of your price range, then you know that one of the tricks up their sleeve is the idea that you "deserve" it.

If we are not careful, we buy into the lie that we deserve just about anything.

Do we though? What we believe about this will be taught in our homes, intentionally or not.

The truth is that we only deserve punishment for our sins, but God sent His son Jesus to this earth to die for you and for me. We DO NOT deserve anything good in the strictest definition of the word. **Rich Mullins**[45] wrote a song called ***"Doubly Good to You."*** A line from the song says:
> "If you find someone that is faithful, if you find someone that's true, thank the Lord. He's been doubly good to you."

And the truth is that sex is good. Nudity is amazing! Our bodies are works of art. If you are able to say that and believe it, you can see that the stewardship God expects of us is not to limit us, but rather to free us. When we believe this, we are free from worry about those things and can eagerly live full lives.

Sex outside of God's design invites bondage, fear, and worry.

THE RELATIONSHIP CONTINUUM

In their book *Soul Virgins,* **Dr. Doug Rosenau** and **Michael Todd Wilson**[46] presented a way to look at dating and courtship that completely revolutionizes the conversation. "Dating" and "courtship" are almost meaningless words in conversation because their definitions vary so much from person to person. By using new terminology, you will be able to help your older child — even adult — navigate relational waters.

If your goal for yourself or a child is a successful, vibrant, and happy marriage, then this is for you.

Picture yourself walking down a path that originates with you being single and unattached and ends at being happily married to your best friend. Do you want to walk on this path with multiple people, only to eventually lose each other in the woods, or would it be wiser to carefully choose only a few (or preferably just one) to walk with you, even if you eventually choose different forks in the path?

Not every love story begins with frienship, but they end up becoming the best of friends along the way, making friendship foundational. Through our interactions in the world we are constantly **CONNECTING**.

Through the process of **CONNECTING**, you are provided with the data you need to know to determine what you like or dislike, your standards, and even your ideal of a life partner. The danger in this stage is that one can set impossible standards that no one can meet.

As you are **CONNECTING**, you will find yourself in conversations that last longer with a few people. Then, eventually, you find those few have narrowed down to one.

This is **COUPLING**.

Some of these relationships will last for a longer season than others. The danger during this stage is to get too physical, and so that must be stewarded carefully. The goal of **COUPLING** is to move with one person toward **COVENANTING** in marriage .

The vocabulary presented here from **Soul Virgins**[47] makes it easy to see the stages of relational life.

CONNECTING is what we do with everyone in your circle — from close friends, to acquaintances, to strangers on the street.

COUPLING is the pairing up that we traditionally define as dating or courting.

COVENANTING is marriage and it is a lifetime commitment.

Now, imagine stepping stones that move you from **CONNECTING** to **COUPLING** and then **COVENANTING**:

The first stepping stone is **FRIENDSHIP**.
Hopefully, you can begin with a friendship as a solid foundation.

A friend that piques your interest and that you intentionally decide to go out with is one that you are **CONSIDERING**. This person has now piqued your curiosity. This step is one of evaluation and requires time, energy, investment, and conversations. The physical aspect of the relationship should be reined in so that it does not cloud your judgment. If this person makes the cut, we would then move into an "engaged-to-be-engaged" step called **CONFIRMING**.

Here you are **CONFIRMING** that you *both* feel certain about continuing to walk down this path together. A ring, future plans, and dreams are discussed.

This is soon followed by the ring in the **COMMITTING** stage. This is engagement and should be short. The time here is spent intentionally preparing for marriage. It is important to remember that this is ONLY THE BEGINNING — the beginning of a beautiful life together in MARRIAGE.

The Relationship Continuum[48] provides us with a broader range of words that allows us to better identify where one is at in a relationship. The boundaries of physical intimacy are different at each stage. Obviously, very minimal physical involvement would be experienced in the **CONNECTING** stage with friends and with those we are **CONSIDERING**. Intercourse and genital focused experiences are reserved for the **COVENANTING** stage of marriage.

I like to say that dating is like marketing, but It needs to be put into its rightful place. Many use this term to say they are "exclusive," but going out on a date should be something you can do with one person tonight and a completely different person tomorrow night without being hurtful.

How can this be? This can happen if those truly in the **CONNECTING** stage have a boundary of no physical touch and have not indulged in long, soul-baring conversations. If this time is used to get to know one another, it can be an experience that allows someone to see what kind of person they enjoy hanging out with. This is best in groups, but can be done one on one if boundaries are in place.

Courtship is a traditional change of status from "single" to "taken." It is exclusive. This person is not seeing anyone else and the young man has asked the young lady's father for permission, though this is considered by many to be archaic. Courtship would include the **CONFIRMING** and **COMMITTING** stages of the Relationship Continuum (this is part of the **COUPLING** stage).[49]

Why does this matter?

You must be proactive in preparing your children to navigate very difficult waters. There will be pressures from every side regarding what they should do, who they should be, and what risks they ought to take. If you have educated them with a game plan and a great vocabulary, they will be able to intentionally navigate relationships and enter marriage with as little baggage as possible.

CHOICES

Now is the time to be deliberate in deciding your sexual ethic. Teaching began with us as parents, but in the end, it is on the shoulders of your twelve-year-old when he is alone at a friend's house.

What will he do when some buddies decide to enter an older sister's room and catch her naked.

It is up to your sixteen-year-old daughter, who desperately wants to be loved, to decide what to do when a boy at school asks for some nude pictures.

It is up to your son to walk away on his own at the park when his group of friends huddle around a screen looking at pornography. In the end, the responsibility is on our children.

The "M" Word

Masturbation — it's a controversial practice and a word that many people cannot even bring themselves to say. I get it. I don't like this word either. It carries with it shame. I prefer to use the term self-stimulation in my counseling practice. Most individuals who do this, do so unconsciously.

Is it wrong? Can it go wrong?

Why has the church used this behavior at times as a determination of someone's commitment to the Christian faith?

Self-stimulation is a private matter that most lie about, but it should be taken out of the shadows and discussed. I have a process that I take young men and women through to help them consciously choose for themselves whether this is good for them or not and if it is contributing to get to where they want to go. Some of those steps are shared throughout this section.

MEDICAL AND CULTURAL CLAIMS

For well over a decade now I have been teaching an undergraduate level course on Human Sexuality. Every year it grows in attendance. The content of the class includes topics and issues that I believe should have been addressed in middle school which is why this book has been written for parents. During one of the classes, I present a theology of masturbation. I do not enter this lightly as I know this issue is one that many students struggle with and are confused about. I spend the first hour presenting the research, the positions held by the medical community, and cultural opinions. Let's begin now with the medical.

The medical community simply states there is no harm caused by self-stimulation. They assert that it is the best way for young people (and children) to learn about how their bodies work and what feels good. It is viewed as the best alternative for release, since it does not include another person and has zero side effects. The medical community goes on to outline the health benefits that regular orgasms have for men and women. Some of the benefits include hay fever relief, lessening of menstrual cramps and pain, lowering the chances of prostate cancer, and aiding with vascular health.

Cultural opinion is also positive, though it is still mainly viewed as a private matter. If no one else is involved, then the sentiment is "no harm, no foul." Go for it. Indulge. Enjoy! Our culture champions self-gratification and so self-stimulation aligns with their ethical considerations.

THE CHURCH'S RESPONSE

The church has also held strong beliefs about masturbation. They include, but are not limited to, "If you do this, you are not a Christian," to, "It is just bad for you," and, "It's a sin." No conversations are allowed. There is just a warning or a threat not to go there. This has proven to be an ineffective strategy.

For many, this activity has been tied to their salvation, and they are living in shame and guilt. I have counseled and been in conversations with men and women that are on the verge of walking away from a call into the ministry — and even their faith — due to the hold that self-stimulation has on their behavior. I have found a very simple solution, but I warn you in advance that this solution is counter intuitive. Many of you will stop reading and be done with me, but I ask you to hang on. Read all the way through to the end. I have seen incredible success and lives transformed by using the approach proposed below.

Be careful with shaming. We know that Satan loves to work in secrecy and in the dark, so be careful with your reactions to your child's actions so that they are less inclined to lie, shut down, and keep things from you.

Be a safe place. **YOU** initiate that safe conversation.

Don't put the responsibility on them to come to you.

This is one of those topics that need adult assistance through *micro-conversations* to bring their actions out of their unconscious operating system and habits and into the forefront of their thinking. This will allow them to make a conscious choice about what is best.

MY APPROACH

Steven walks into my office. He is twenty years old and feels trapped. He has been taught that masturbation is sin and also bad for him. As we begin, I open our conversation to this embarrassing topic through disarming comments that aim to teach and educate. First, I compare the things he has been taught about self-stimulation to medical research. I ask him questions like, "So what? What's the big deal? Does anyone know or care? Why does this stress you out to the point of such depression or frustration?" I am hoping to move him toward a new view of his choice to stimulate himself to orgasm. What I find is that most men and women fall into these habits unconsciously and habitually. I want to bring it to his conscious reasoning. Why does he (or she) do this? What is the purpose? What payoff does he (or she) get out of it?

After he is a bit more relaxed about the topic, I begin to lead him down a path toward viewing self-stimulation as amoral and, without question, NOT sinful. Perhaps even acceptable. Why do I do this? I do this because I want HIM to determine the kind of impact it is having on his life. It does not work for me, or anyone else, to tell him that it is harmful, if he does not accept it and choose to live with that truth. So, as I walk him towards it being one hundred percent okay, I begin to drop hints that suggest a new narrative:

What if self-stimulation is actually moving you further away from what you say you truly want? What if, when you self-stimulate while thinking about a person you just met at church, school, or the grocery store, this activity is taking you further away from getting to know them and building a real relationship with them? Maybe this is not such a good idea after all (a conscious choice). At this point, I begin looking for their greater goal in life and relationships. I want them to come to a point of consciously choosing NOT to engage in this behavior, but I cannot go there immediately and achieve this outcome.

When I talk to some people about masturbation, I tell them to stop stressing about it and enjoy it. It is a longer conversation than that, but I am blown away at how many come back a few weeks later and report that by being given permission to enjoy it, but also being made aware of the potential impact this can and will have on real relationships, they were less tempted and/or chose not engage in that behavior any longer. This is a powerful testimony to the importance of honest conversation.

You and I do not react well to rules, laws, and regulations that make no sense to us. However, most of us are willing to comply with a boundary when we understand why it is there. I pray that the Lord will bless you as you lead your children in the difficult conversations that they so desperately need.

Addressing Past Trauma

Earlier, we discussed the impact trauma has on us, and how shame devolves into hate, or contempt, and how this is a path of death. Right now, I want you to focus on your child. This gift from God is someone you are to protect at all costs. No harm should ever befall them. Is this a reality you can truly enforce? No, it is not. It is a setup for failure.

Most parents believe that their child is free of sexual thoughts and if they can just keep them from being "exposed" to something, they will be protected. However, in my counseling experience, I see over and over that the child who was "protected" sought out pornography, or they began experimenting sexually with their friends or siblings and now border on being labeled as a perpetrator. This is avoidable.

YOU must prepare your children for the real world. As you have seen throughout this book, I believe that most parents err on the side of too little, too late. We must be preemptive.

The statistics on exposure to pornography and engagement in first sexual experiences ought to terrify us. This feeling ought to propel us to begin hard conversations and protect them by preparing them.

It is wise and good to attempt to protect your children while they are in your home and in your presence. The reality though is that they are going to leave your presence. It is then that I see that what parents have attempted to do as a protection ends up backfiring as their child is not prepared when they are confronted with potential danger.

When your child leaves home and goes to preschool, are they prepared for the realities they will face — those with different views, different beliefs, gender issues, bullying, and more?

When your child joins that sports team, are they prepared for the locker room talk, comparison, and not being the best?

Whether your child is in a private, public, or homeschool setting, these conversations matter. Many of the stories I hear are of abuse and lines that were crossed at a church camp, or at a fellow Christian's home with their "protected" kids. Anyone and everyone can become curious, but that curiosity needs guidance. An excellent resource for you to consider is **Dr. Peter Levine's** book *Trauma-Proofing Your Kids*.[50]

BUILDING RESILIENCE

Dr. Peter Levine[51] suggests that trauma is magnified in a person by the level of shutdown in a terrifying experience. We know that babies are affected by traumatic events, such as a lack of love, touch, safety, nourishment, etc. This trauma is stored — even trapped — in the body. It lives there throughout a lifetime. Learning to minimize its power and effect is what is called **"trauma-proofing."**

This can be accomplished by **"building resilience"** in our children from an early age — even as young as infancy.

The recipe for building resilience is the level of know-how to fight or flee rather than freezing.

Fighting and fleeing expend the adrenaline and physical energy pent up in response to a threat or potential trauma, regardless of our age.

Freezing is a survival mechanism that leads us through the experience, but that energy remains pent up inside our physical body. This energy penetrates throughout our bodies, which is manifested in physical and mental health difficulties throughout our lives.

So, **what is "building resilience?"** This is your child's ability to "rebound" after something activates the fight/flight/freeze mechanism. Think of an event — whether it is an actual threat or a perceived one — as knocking your child off balance. Their equilibrium is lost. The quicker that they can return to their baseline, the better off they will be. The goal is to learn this process for yourself. To find yourself able to respond to an event with ease and without excessive reaction is an empowering feeling. Not everyone will get to this point, but the goal is to **be more self-aware** as to how you respoind. Seeing that no matter how freaked out you get your body always calms down eventually, can make the worst of a situation tolerable because you know that you will naturally calm down in a moment or two. This is powerful. When we learn this as adults it is powerful. For our children to get this at a young age is empowering and freeing for them.

Think about it this way: your nervous system is always communicating to your child's nervous system. That sounds weird, doesn't it? What happens though when your child falls?

They tend to look to you as to how they should react. If you freak out, they freak out. If you are calm, they are more likely to be calm or to get their more quickly. Many parents make small issues huge by their reaction, or better said, their over-reaction. It is one thing to be able to eventually calm yourself. It is another one to know how to experience something uncomfortable and not let it get the best of you.

A concept that I love from **Dr. Levine**,[52] as well as other authors on healing trauma, is that of the **"felt sense."** We have thoughts and feelings about a situation. We also have physical sensations with each experience. Putting words to these physical reactions can be powerful, empowering, and freeing. You may freak out, but choose to not over-react. You may feel something, but, based on your physical sensations, reinterpret what you felt. You can think something and, based on the physical sensations, change your relationship with the event itself. This is powerful stuff.

Building resilience in your children includes a calming presence from us as their caregivers. They are looking to us for our reactions and they in turn react to us, almost intuitively. Our brains are complex and include the ability to feel, think, and use the felt sense in a way that better informs our bodies as to the reality of an event. This allows us to regain equilibrium more quickly, or maintain control in the face of potential threats, hurt, fear, or pain.

WHAT TO DO IN THE FACE OF POTENTIAL HARM

Jenny finds herself stressing out over an upcoming test. She quickly remembers though that she has a choice as to how much she lets this train run away in her head. She assesses the worst-case scenarios, notices her body sensations, and considers her thoughts and feelings. She sees her reaction as valid due to the lack of time she spent studying. She recognizes that the speed of her heart rate is an overreaction and that catastrophizing is unhelpful. Almost immediately, she finds her physical body calming down. She has averted a panic attack, similar to dozens of others she used to have over everything around her. She has learned to be resilient. She has learned to stay inquisitive and curious about her responses, rather than over-reacting and adding fuel to the fire, which only encouraged a full-blown panic response in the past.

Ken is a police officer who has found himself in some tough moments where fear and panic began to enter his system. He has learned how to respond. He begins by noticing his body and its reactions first. He then assesses the situation as to the validity of his initial reaction to the potential threat. Is it real or only perceived? He then reassesses his physical reactions, and if they are unnecessary, finds himself calming down quickly. However, if they are valid, he finds himself able to shift in his reaction toward the situation and respond appropriately rather than having his physiology take over. This is resilience. He maintains control more often than not. He can think more clearly in those moments. He finds himself more calm in the face of danger, whether real or not.

What do we do for our children? We can help them tap into this innate ability. We are wired to respond to danger. We also have the ability to perform under stress.

The key as parents, ironically, is to allow situations in your child's life to occur so that you can coach them through a response.

Some of these will be after the fact, having less impact, but still helping them learn. Some though, we can catch as they happen and have a powerful teachable moment. The goal is that our children learn they have more choices than they realize when it feels like their bodies or their brains are being hijacked and they feel out of control. This does not have to be the default. Success breeds success. The next time they can find control and quickly choose well in less time. **Listening and paying attention to physical sensations is a critical skill.**

Our reactions as caregivers are paramount for their success. Helping your child put language to their experiences, feelings, and physical reactions is empowering. **Rest is critical.** Providing a safe place to process their reactions after the fact becomes a learning experience. Giving your child the space and freedom to feel is priceless.

An effective tool for children and teens who have experienced trauma is the **intentional use of play.** They are able to process what they've experienced by playing it out. This can be done via art, music, toys, games, etc. You may be able to use these tools as a parent to draw out their feelings and reactions to a situation.

As I mentioned earlier in this book, one approach that we took with our children when they were young was to talk with them after they had been with a babysitter. We would ask them if their babysitter had touched them in their private areas or asked them to do anything that they thought was weird. We were not necessarily expecting an honest response as those experiences often bring on shame and silence. We were looking for a different physical reaction to the question than the baseline of the other thirty times they were asked. (We also communicated to our sitters that we always asked these questions so that they would not feel singled out and also to hopefully prevent anything from ever happening). We attempted to pay attention to whether they paused, averted their eyes, or squirmed in coming up with their response. This is a technique you might want to use yourself. It is uncomfortable, but it is saying each time that you are choosing to be a safe place to share this information, but this also means you MUST choose to be a safe place.

PREPARING THEM WELL

From birth to age five, your child is absorbing the **ENERGY** you put out in your reactions, passions, and emotional and spiritual health. This time of life is all about their safety and letting them know they have people they can trust. Most children are overwhelmingly trusting. Help them hang onto that by being a trusted, stable presence in their life.

Between the ages of six and ten, your child is absorbing the **CULTURE** of your home. They are already beginning to separate from you a bit. They want — and need — opportunities for freedom. They need to experience pain, pleasure, loss, fear, joy — the range of human emotions. **They learn to worship what you worship,** see the world through your eyes, and react to their interpretation of the world in tangible ways over the following years.

The ages of eleven to seventeen welcome the peak of sexual interest and curiosity. This also brings along with it a stronger separation from caregivers and a struggle with their identity. They ask questions like:

"Who am I?"

"What do I stand for?" and

"Where am I going?"

This age is when most begin to date, and therefore they have an incredible need for stewardship and a strong biblical sexual ethic — an ETHOS. **Having "the talk" now is usually pointless.**

When does harm enter their story? Unfortunately, it can be present at any of these ages. Preparation is the key. **Resilience** and the ability NOT to freeze is crucial.

It is imperative that your children have the skills they need for self-regulation and knowing how to fight or to flee. You are leading them, whether you realize it or not, and whether you are intentional or not. You are their primary guide.

This is more than a request. This is a call to step up and lead confidently and intentionally from a position of knowledge as you prepare yourself through education, which will give your children a better chance of success.

Be THAT parent.

Love them THAT much.

Have THOSE *micro-conversations*.

Prepare them well.

The world is waiting.

I Can't Say That!

CHAPTER 9

BUILDING YOUR PERSONAL ETHOS

We have walked through a lot and you are probably wondering how to bring this home and make it yours. Your own personal ETHOS was set in place when you were young, just as it is being set now in the lives and hearts of your children. This process will likely involve pruning for you as you examine why you believe (or don't believe) certain things. You will find that you are securing some things and letting others go. You are adding information, challenging old assumptions, and allowing "iron to sharpen iron" (Proverbs 27:17, NLT).

A word of caution is necessary here though: **be discerning as to who you listen to and who you elevate as an authority.** In this chapter, I want you to be able to put some of these things down in writing. This will help you tremendously to pass them on intentionally to your children and family.

A biblical sexual ethic — your ETHOS — must include a theology of sex, marriage, and a conviction that your role as a parent is one of leadership in this area. If you believe that being a leader means that you are the ultimate authority in all things and you are NOT sensitive to the needs, opinions, and view of others, your life will bear the fruit from this approach. If, on the other hand, you believe that you CAN'T tell your kids the truth as you understand it from God's Word, then your opinion will NOT carry weight, and if you never speak up, stand up, or fight for anything, your legacy will bear these fruits.

I hope that your commitment will be to think through these issues, study God's Word, and be able to articulate what you believe and why you believe it to your children through multiple *micro-conversations* that will bear good fruit. Commit to living by your biblical sexual ethic and lead by example with confidence.

Ecclesiastes 3:22 puts our work into perspective:
"So I saw that there is nothing better for people than to be happy in their work. That is our lot in life. And no one can bring us back to see what happens after we die" (NLT).

Invest in your most important job—raising your children—preparing them.

Building My Personal ETHOS

Your Personal ETHOS — or belief system — must have a foundation. **A first step will be to decide if that will be tradition, your own personal experiences, or God's Word.** Your actions prove which one guides you at any given moment or decision point.

Are you guided more by what others think of you?
Are you motivated by fear due to your own experiences of traumatic events?

Deciding to make God's Word your foundation will require that you make difficult decisions. Some of these will be unpopular—not only to other parents in your community, but especially to your children. This is part of the reason that I am intent on having these *micro-conversations* with your child at a younger age than you probably think is necessary. This provides a greater chance that your child will adopt your biblical sexual ethic as their own and makes it less likely that they will fight you on unpopular cultural stances. They will understand your view and be more willing to go along with your desire for them if it is also their desire for themselves. This is a beautiful dance that, if played well by starting early, can make the adolescent years a time of relationship and adventure with your children as you carefully and intentionally prepare them to launch into the world.

This MUST be the goal.
They cannot stay with you forever—it harms them and you.
They need independence.
They need room to spread their wings and fly, to fall, and then pick themselves up and try again.

Your priorities regarding dating, sex, and marriage for your children must be addressed when they are in their formative years.

You can do this!

SETTING THE STAGE FOR SUCCESS (IT STARTS WITH YOU)

As you process all that you have read so far, what are some places where you feel stuck?
What are some questions that emerge?

As you think about your son and/or daughter dating, having sex, marrying, being a spouse and becoming a parent, what are the primary concerns that you have for them?

Can you clearly see the path that you desire for them has the least amount of pain and is full of joy, strength of character, and healthy relationships?

Most of you want to provide this or you wouldn't be reading this book. Most parents want to spare their children from any pain or trauma. The truth though is that we cannot. So, let's prepare them. Let's equip them. Let's describe the road that is before them so that they will avoid pitfalls and side trails and choose, on their own, to stay on the path.

YOUR LIVING ETHOS

If your foundation is Scripture — God's Word — you can find clarity on many issues, although there will be difficulty as you navigate with your child how to talk about those things, especially if they or someone they care about is struggling. Let's review.

Gender:
Scripture is clear about God creating humans as male and female. Scripture is clear about the Lord calling them to come together and multiply (Genesis 1:27-28; 1:15-24). Unless you or your child was born with ambiguous genitalia, also known as intersex, you are either male or female. Remember though that you are unique in your design as a male or female. Many of the battles that people are facing today are not actually against their gender, but against what society has said a man or woman should look like or act like.

Pornography:

Research shows that pornography is damaging to the heart, head and relationships. It also exploits those men and women in the videos and images. Scripture is clear on this one. Recent studies show an increase of men in their twenties with erectile dysfunction due to pornography use.[53] WOW! This is avoidable. There is no place for it inside or outside of marriage. If you want your marriage to thrive, say no! If you want to be married and stay married one day, say no! If you are content being single, but desire to treat others with respect, then say no!

Dating:

When should your child begin dating? Great question. If we look to Scripture, you will see that it does not address dating. A rule of thumb is to remember the admonition of Scripture that:

> "there must not be even a hint of sexual immorality, or of any kind of impurity, or of greed, because these are improper for God's holy people" (Ephesians 5:3, NIV).

There is no magic age, but dating should wait until they can bear the weight of another person's heart and be responsible for the outcomes of a physical relationship. If they are not at an age where marriage is a consideration or a possibility, then it is my opinion that they are playing with fire. This is discussed in greater depth in chapter eight.

Marriage:

The Lord says:

> "Give honor to marriage, and remain faithful to one another in marriage. God will surely judge people who are immoral and those who commit adultery" (Hebrews 13:4, NLT).

Scripture is also clear that this covenant is between a man and a woman (Genesis 1:18-25; Matthew 19:1-9; 1 Corinthians 7). The purpose of marriage and family is the raising up of the next generation to know God and honor Him (Psalms 18:5-7).

Marriage is hard, but it is an incredible blessing not to walk through life alone. What great care God has for us! Yes, we live in a broken world that has led many into more than one marriage after the dissolution of a previous marriage. God is a God of grace. He restores. He renews. Sexuality is to be stewarded in marriage just as it is during your single days. Marriage is the only setting in which the physical activity that has the potential to bring life into this world ought to be experienced. Does that mean all other sexual activity is acceptable outside of marriage? The Lord says:

> "God's will is for you to be holy, so stay away from all sexual sin. Then each of you will control his own body and live in holiness and honor—not in lustful passion like the pagans who do not know God and his ways. Never harm or cheat a fellow believer in this matter by violating his wife, for the Lord avenges all such sins, as we have solemnly warned you before" (1 Thessalonians 4:3-6, NLT).

The only place for sexual intimacy is within marriage.

Sex:
Sex (intercourse) is primarily meant to serve as the place where the sperm and egg are brought together to create new life. Thankfully, that doesn't happen every time a man and woman come together! Sex — and by that I mean genital play — is also meant to be a pleasure enjoyed by a man and woman within the safety and boundaries of marriage. Research shows that those in a monogamous relationship, whether they married or not are exponentially more likely to NOT have to worry about sexually transmitted infections. Sex is meant to be beautiful. Sex is meant to be holy, a sacrament. Sex is also meant to be a regular part of marriage. This serves as protection against the temptations that abound. It is an incredible source of pleasure as well. Procreation is a natural result, but waits in God's timing.

Technology:
These tools need to be stewarded. They are not expensive toys! Teach your children about what is appropriate to view and post online. These tools are not the enemy, but Satan sure knows how to use them. Talk to them about cyberbullying and internet safety.

Idols:
Be careful who or what you raise up to be worshipped. There is to be ONLY ONE GOD. We do not always do this intentionally, but what we prioritize as a family is often evident in kids' lives. Be cognizant of what could become an idol. Do not let it distract you from the One who truly deserves our worship and your involvement in a local church, which is the Body and bride of Christ (Hebrews 10:23-25; 1 Corinthians 12). You and your children need the Body of Christ and the body needs you.

YOUR ASSIGNMENT

Now, it is your turn to make this YOURS.

Start with Scripture listed here, but examine them for yourself.

Pray that the Lord will instruct you in both the meaning of the scriptures, and how you and your family should live this out.

If you are married, this is best done as a couple so that you are both on the same page and you can lead your family intentionally together.

I Have A Plan

You are getting closer to more engaging and quality *micro-conversations* that will yield results. Remember that this is about the long game and the results might not be seen right away. You are planting seeds. You are beginning dialogue when they are younger, so that when they are older and asking harder questions, they have a good understanding of where you stand.

A few months ago, my twelve-year-old son asked me, "So, when can I begin dating?"

My response to him was:
"Remember when we went through '*Passport to Purity*'?[54] You signed over that decision to me, and I told you that the best time is your junior or senior year of college. Do you remember why?"

He did remember. Can I be responsible for her heart? Can I drive? Can I afford dinner and a movie? Can I afford a ring? Am I ready to have a baby within a few years of beginning dating?

He already knew my answer though. We have been discussing this for years and he even attends many of my college classes and teaching at churches on the subject. He needed some affirmation. Why? He hears a very different message around him and he also has internal drives and desires he is learning to steward.

I continued, "This is the time to have amazing relationships without getting hung up on titles. Get to know a lot of different young ladies, learn what you like and do not like. Have fun with friends, grow, mature, have fun, live by boundaries. Then when you are able to walk into a relationship, make it great, and have little to no baggage to carry into marriage."

He got it! Why?

We have had this discussion multiple times.
We go back to it.
We expand on it.
He has new questions about it.
This is a beautiful exchange. Remember who is responsible, though, for these decisions and to steward his dating, sexual, and relational self?

He is. Your child is. NOT YOU!

MY THEOLOGY OF SEX

Is sex (intercourse) okay between two consenting adults? A better question is whether this is wise?

Another question is whether this is something that will separate us from God. I want you to be able to articulate answers to questions like these. You are preparing yourself to lead your children through difficult questions in a challenging world that lives by a different ethic.

Telling them, "NO," or, "It's bad," is not helpful. Sometimes, it is even abusive. Sex and sexuality are beautiful parts of all of us, single and married alike. Let's raise sons and daughters that see it this way and make wise decisions with their bodies, with what they look at, and how they live in community with others.

Write out Scripture and other ideas and resources that inform your ETHOS on Sex.

Further questions can be found in the workbook that complements this book.

Do you have questions? Write them down.

Think through them. Wrestle with them. Be confident when you come to a conclusion because you know you have done the work of prayerfully studying Scripture and understand the bigger picture of God's design.

Be careful that your own experience is not the only thing forming your beliefs. Listen to what others say, but be careful who you listen to. Some are truly seeking to understand and apply Scripture. Others are looking out for their own good. Some are neutral and deserve our attention and reflection, as we filter them through other parts of Scripture and God's desire for our best.

MY THEOLOGY OF MARRIAGE

Marriage is not a right. Marriage is a sacred commitment and a privilege that should NOT be entered into lightly. It is hard. It doubles both your joy and your burdens. Companionship is an incredible gift which helps explain why there is such a large push in our culture to redefine marriage.

Marriage is two broken people choosing to bind their lives, souls, and bodies to go through life together. Marriage is give and take. It is FULL of dying to yourself. It is NOT for the faint of heart. Marriage is a place to wrestle with hard things, disagree, fight, make up, forgive, be broken, hurt, and heal. It is a safe place for couples as they go through both beautiful and difficult times. It is also the only place where children truly thrive. The more we learn about human development, the more we recognize the importance of engaged parents, the role of the father, and the models of both masculinity and femininity. It is where children first learn about leadership, cooperation, forgiveness, and grace.

There are troubling teachings in some churches regarding headship and authority, submission, and the roles of a husband and wife in marriage. As I study Scripture, I see no indication that the model of a husband dominating his wife to the point where she has no voice and must obey is what Jesus intends for marriage to look like. His example is one of putting His bride before Himself.

What is your theology of marriage?

Write out the beliefs you have about marriage.

What is your framework based on?
Does your framework consider the totality of Scripture or are they cherry-picked to make you more comfortable?
Can you teach this to your children confidently?
Are you a cynic? A romantic? Are you grounded in the truth?

What are some questions that come to mind as you think about your marriage?
What has been your experience with marriage?
What are your fears?
What concerns do you have for your children's future?

Write them down and prayerfully wrestle with them. Apply Scripture to your situation. Again, be aware of the sexual ethic and respect for Scripture that others have as you decide who to listen to for advice on marriage.

Further questions can be found in the workbook.

MY BELIEF SYSTEM OF LEADERSHIP AS A PARENT

Finally, let's discuss you as a parent. You may be doing this alone or with a partner. You may be in your first marriage, never married, or on a second or third marriage.

Who are you as a parent?
Are you strong? Are you tender? Can you do both?

One of the beliefs I have come to hold after years of counseling practice and teaching, is that most single parents, regardless of whether they are the mother or father, believe that they must be both mom and dad in their children's lives. This is not true and can even cause more damage to their children. What I have come to believe is that what they need most from you is to be the best mom or dad that you can be. You are not and will never be the opposite gender. Stop pretending you can be all things to everyone.

If you are a single mom, you need to get your children around a healthy male influence. If you are a single dad, you need to get your children around a healthy female influence. There is already an irreplaceable loss here. Acknowledge that loss and grieve over what that means. Be proactive and intentional to put positive influences in your children's lives. This is where the Body of Christ can come alongside you if they know your needs.

This is also true though for families with two parents. As men and women, we each fall short of who we should be in our children's lives. We need community. For some families, they put their kids in school, a sport, or an extra-curricular activity and call it good — influence in place. Check. Do not do this blindly though. What is the worldview of those running these activities? Are they leading your child well?

I hear testimonies from students that there were key influencers—both for good and bad—in their developmental years. Outside of parents — coaches, youth pastors, and teachers are mentioned the most often. I want you, as a parent, to be proactive in building a band of influencers around your children when they are young. You choose them — not your child! Be deliberate and thoughtful.

Interestingly, we have built this with our children via Scouting with our sons, and American Heritage Girls with our daughter. I am honored to be invited into the lives of the other families and become an influence on other boys' lives. I often tell my sons that if they have a question or problem that they don't want to talk to me about, I hope they will go to one of the other dads in our Scout group. I also tell them that they will sometimes find themselves jealous because I am helping, correcting, and encouraging another boy. I want them to know that I am doing what I want other parents to do for them.

At our summer campout, which was seven days long, I only spoke with my son about four times. I was present, but I kept my distance. I had several conversations with many of the other boys. I was also building relationships with the other dads, which is critical for my own health and well-being. I was there though when my son had a break down, but quickly removed myself again after calming him down, so that he could figure out a solution on his own. We should want to raise up men and women that have the grit, strength, and security to march to a different drum.

I want my children to know how to face adversity, and not back down. I also want them to have the wisdom to look at potential conflict and walk away.

Will I, as the parent, be there for each one? Nope. But my teaching, training, and preparation will be, whether it was intentional or not. Each of our children walk into problems with the training we gave them. Let's lead with integrity, with strength, and with tenderness. You are NOT alone, but, you ARE a leader! You are a parent, which is probably the most important calling on your life. Lead confidently. Lead with integrity.

I Commit To Living By A Plan

Okay, that was a lot! Do you commit to leading with purpose? Do you commit to entering difficult conversations? For example:

You must discuss with your daughter and prepare her for her period. Her menstrual cycle could begin when she is ten or eleven years old. Don't let it surprise her and make her think she is dying. Prepare her.

Your son will experience an erection and, realizing what the trigger was, almost always feel embarrassment and shame. Prepare him. *Micro-conversations* are essential for this. Lead by staying ahead of your children. I am a resource to you if you are ever stuck. Do not hesitate to reach out to me, your pastor, or another Christian counselor.

I LEAD BY EXAMPLE

Be open to talking about things, and be honest about how hard it is. Carefully share your story of mistakes, heartaches, and pains. Be vulnerable. If you want your children to grow up uncommunicative, uninformed, or misinformed (via the internet and peers), do not have any of the conversations I have labored to outline in this book. This is NOT easy as it takes a lot out of us. Remember that we have access to be the Body of Christ.

I have found that I have a unique passion, training, and expertise that allows me to partner with you and help you enter these hard places. Be an example to your children of what you want them to be. You are an example already, whether you want to be or not, so you should be intentional and thoughtful as you guide them.

I LEAD WITH ASSERTIVENESS

When my son first asked about babies, we got a book off the shelf on that subject and read it. He ran off and it appeared that it didn't register. But it did. A few months later, he asked a more pointed question and my wife passed the conversation off to me. I got the same book out and the sex part registered. Suddenly, he understood that the penis had to go inside the girl for the sperm and egg to meet. "GROSSSS!" was his response, and five seconds later he was playing with Legos and seemingly oblivious. He wasn't though and neither are your children. **They are always processing what they see and hear.** A few more weeks passed and our next few conversations — *micro-conversations* — went deeper fast.

He showed me that he was ready and we needed to talk about it. It was earlier than I expected to have this conversation. By giving him this information, I was giving him a responsibility to steward the information wisely. Many parents fear that their child will take this information to school and share it with everyone. That is a valid concern. Part of the conversation should be training them to have discernment and to be careful where and with whom they discuss these things. But, if we do not prepare them, they will learn it from the kid at school that learned it somewhere else and is probably full of misinformation.

Go there. Lead. Prepare. Be gracious. Be patient. And remember — *micro-conversations*, not lectures!

I LEAD WITH CONFIDENCE

You can lead with confidence.

What gives you confidence? Knowing what you believe and why you believe it.
Should your sixteen-year-old start dating?

What do you believe? You need to know. I am here to help, along with a host of other leaders in this field that are called, trained, and living from a biblical sexual ethic.

I met with a family recently about their son. I told them I would be glad to meet with their son and discuss some of these hard things, as I already do with college aged students, but that I prefer to empower them to have these conversations themselves. They are on the front lines. They need tools and skills to have these conversations late at night and at times when a "professional" is not available to pop in and have a chat.

You can do this. You never need to have all the answers. Teach your children that they will always be growing and learning. Be an example of a life-long learner that seeks out answers and comes back to them with those answers. These are the lifesaving *micro-conversations* that will change your children's futures.

I Can't Say That!

CHAPTER 10

THE POWER AND IMPORTANCE OF COMMUNITY

Ken and Jill are parents that have been on this same journey with their kids that you are on now. They began their journey when their son, who was not yet a teenager, began acting out sexually, and they came in for counseling. I had the honor of walking with this young man through much of the material presented in this book. I talked with him about pornography, the "M" word, and helped him develop a biblical sexual ethic. The purpose of these conversations was to empower him to consciously choose what he would do in all situations rather than acting unconsciously. I also had the opportunity to walk his parents through this process as well so that they were equipped to lead their other children toward a biblical sexual ethic. They need to have their own personal development of an ETHOS that is grounded in God's Word and realistic about preparing them for the world outside their home.

Sam and Carolina are parents that have grown children, but saw them make unwise decisions when they were in their teens and their twenties. Now, their children are all married and they have the honor of being Grammy and Pappy. They realized that since they had not talked with their children about issues surrounding sexuality, their children were now following in their footsteps and not talking with their grandchildren. They began to have *micro-conversations* with their grandchildren as they encountered various situations and this began to plant seeds in their hearts and minds. This led their grandchildren to ask hard questions at home to their parents, which led them to examine their own sexual ethic — their ETHOS — and what they lacked when they were growing up. They empowered themselves as adults with knowledge and followed the example of their parents. They are grateful that their parents cared enough to get involved and motivated them to talk with their children because they were then prepared when they had to walk through some traumatic incidents and experiences with their children. Their parents, **Sam and Carolina**, took a risk for their grandkids' sake and it paid off greatly.

As you are reading or listening to this, my hope is that you are being transformed.

I hope you have been encouraged and motivated to dive into *micro-conversations* with your children. These will absolutely change the course of their lives forever. I do not make this statement lightly.

You are engaging in a battle for your children.

By implementing these short talks with your children, which seem insignificant at the time, you establish the belief that you can and will give them real, raw, and honest answers. They will face heartache and heartbreak. They will experience love and loss.

If you want to know what is going on in their hearts as they get older, you must start investing in it when they are young.

Reminders And Challenges

Parenting was never meant to be a solo sport. If you are a single parent, I know that you are carrying a huge weight on your shoulders. **Raising young men and women that honor God and make confident, wise decisions is done in community.** Please do your best to find a community within your church that will come alongside you to pray for your family and help you in tangible ways as well.

As a parent, how you view your children will impact how you lead. For some, becoming a mom or dad was a difficult and long path, and you hold that title with honor. Some of you landed here by accident.

Does God play games or make mistakes?

No, He doesn't. However you earned the title of mom or dad, wear it proudly. You have been entrusted with a precious gift.

YOUR KIDS ARE GIFTS — IT IS ALL ABOUT STEWARDSHIP

Jeffrey is a handful. He is loud and eager to answer. He is energetic and funny. He is curious and wild. He gets himself into trouble with his impulsivity.

Sarah is a shy, quiet young lady. She does not engage with others. She retreats from relationships. She struggles with her thoughts, but does not let anyone know.

Each of your children are gifts from God. Their uniqueness and idiosyncrasies are part of God's design. He does NOT make mistakes. We, as parents, spouses, and friends, make mistakes in every role we play. Our God does not. Guiding your child's personality is part of the journey. Their emotions and behavior can be overwhelming and even maddening.

Your son is now carrying the title of perpetrator or molester. He needs you. He needs to bear responsibility, but he also needs to know that he is still lovable — to you and God — and has hope for the future.

Your daughter has been molested. She needs you. She needs to know how to process what has happened and that she is worth fighting for. She needs to know that she still has a bright future.

How do you steward your own sexuality, gender, and temptations?

How you manage these will impact how you are able to help your children when they need you most. If you are struggling in this area, please get help. The best gift that you can give your children is honesty regarding your mistakes and then asking for their forgiveness.

They need to see confession, repentance, and forgiveness modeled more than they need a perfect mom or dad.

This is all about stewardship.

The responsibilities of parenting go beyond food, shelter, and clothing. We have a responsibility to educate and prepare them for the world. We have a responsibility to model for them what stewarding sexuality looks like when we live with a biblical sexual ethic.

BE PROACTIVE AND PREVENTATIVE

Think of parenting as preparing them for battle. I want to remind you over and over that it begins with us.

Are we responsible for our children's decisions?

No, we are not. They have free will. They are their own people. They grow up, face temptations, and make their own decisions. As they enter different life stages and the struggles that come with each, they are accountable for their own decisions. I do not know a good parent out there that does not take ownership in some way for their children's bad decisions. We must remember that it is part of our job to pray as we prepare them.

So, my question to you is have you prepared them for whatever may come?

Did you discuss stranger danger and prepare them for the nine percent chance of abuse from a stranger, but never prepare them to say, "NO," and stand up for themselves when a sibling, uncle, babysitter, or family friend asks them to take their clothes off or do something sexual?

I often hear from parents, "But I had those conversations with my child!" However, their children say they did not have these conversations. What is the disconnect? The disconnect comes from the form of "the talk" as opposed to *micro-conversations*. "The talk" is usually an information dump that is given too late to have a meaningful impact on building a child's sexual ethic — their ETHOS.

Micro-conversations invite dialogue, two-way conversation, and relationship. It is being proactive in dropping truths carefully into your child's life that they then choose to pick up and live out. Their decisions are their responsibility once you have prepared them. If you have "the talk," there is a good chance that it will not settle into your child's heart. If you are intentional over the years, proactive and intentional to invite arguments and conversation through relationship with them, you have done well! Regardless of the choices your child makes, you have fulfilled your responsibility by training up your child in the way they should go (Proverbs 22:6, NKJV)

.

BE CONFIDENT

A key part of being confident is knowledge. There aren't many people, especially men, that love reading books about marriage, trauma, parenting, sexuality, and shame. You each have your own passions, interests, skills, and areas of expertise. Share these with others by helping them. Help someone fix something if you are great at fixing things. Help someone plan something if that is your skill set. This book is my attempt to share my skill set and knowledge with you. I want to help as many families as possible change their family tree.

Community

Sam and Kelly have found themselves struggling with their sixteen-year-old son. The battles, the stress, and the tears are devastating to them both. The impact on their marriage has been earthshattering. Their saving grace has been their community. They attend a large church where they were lost in the crowd for a long time. But now, within that community, they have formed friendships that have become their lifeline as they now have peers to bounce ideas off and shoulders to cry on if needed. Two families in their group have been through similar struggles with their own children and have been a tremendous source of encouragement as they share the tools they have picked up over the years.

My wife and I have seen the power of community throughout our lives, even before we were married. Before I met my wife, people from my Sunday School class would pick me up and take me to doctors' appointments when I was battling with my health. Throughout our marriage, our church community and friends have been an incredible support through health scares, loneliness, the births of our children, and when we had to make hard decisions. For me, my biker (motorcycle) friends have been a source of friendship, spiritual encouragement, and an example of how to live as imperfect men of God. Our life stage now finds our community coming from the relationships we have with parents of our children's friends at our church's Boy Scout and American Heritage Girls troops.

Think about it — who do you spend the most time around?

What are those people's beliefs and values?

Do you want to be like them?

Be intentional about community.

This means you will need to be very thoughtful about what you commit to, how much time it will take, and the impact it will have on your family dynamic. You do not have to say yes to everything. You do not have to do whatever your children express an interest in.

Be smart as a family.

Be careful that you are not being pulled in twenty different directions either. Like we tell our children, we become like the people we spend time with.

WE WERE NEVER MEANT TO DO THIS ALONE

Parenting was never meant to be a solo sport. I am humbled when I see single moms that are bearing all that weight day in and day out. We are stubborn people. We struggle to ask for and receive help. We all have pride issues. Some of us have servant issues. We do not receive well — or we do not give well. Where are you on that spectrum?

Marriage was not meant to be two people banding together and then disappearing from the world. Your marriage needs input and challenge from friends and others to grow. Men— you need good, godly men in your life. I am currently writing this while on a campout with my oldest son's Boy Scouts troop. There are three other dads here that I love spending time with whenever I get the chance. I love that my son will feel comfortable going to them if he is struggling and that their sons might come to me.

That is community — that is the Body of Christ.

Ladies — you need women in your life. You need someone that can encourage you as a wife, mom, and in your career aspirations and priorities. We ALL need mentors and mentees.

Be intentional to build relationships in which you are serving others. There is always someone that can benefit from knowing you and learning from your experiences and what the Lord is teaching you.

Times of crisis will reveal who your friends are like nothing else. Many years ago, I was lying in a hospital bed following a motorcycle wreck. A car had pulled out in front of me and I t-boned it with my six-year-old son on the seat behind me. Thankfully, he wasn't hurt at all — not even a bruise! I remember looking at the three men standing there, who had taken care of my wife, kids, and bike, before they were there with me. I said, "Man, it stinks to have to have this happen to be reminded of those that love us."

SEEK COMMUNITY (FIND)

The first place that I would recommend you look for community is in a local faith community. What characteristic is the most important to you in bonding to another person or group of people? Is it personality, a common hobby, faith, life stage? These can be the glue that holds a beginning friendship together.

Think about a group of parents that gather together to cheer on their son or daughter in their sport. The common thread that unites these parents is usually the age of their kids and their children's mutual interest in that sport. There is often not much else. This is unfortunate and it is often an unhealthy community. Oftentimes, groups like this bond together when they are trying to get a coach fired, or they are focused on a common problem and they feed each other's negativity. Relationships like this will not help you when you are in a crisis. However, a group of parents can also realize that while they may have initially met through their children's sport, they share many other things in common and they can be a source of encouragement to their kids, each other, their teams, and bring the light of Christ where He may not have been before.

I recently went on a motorcycle trip with a group of men from a local church. I knew a few of them from a previous trip five years earlier. The excuse to get together was our love and enthusiasm for motorcycles. The real reason for our excursion over the Cascades and into the high desert of

Eastern Oregon though was a shared faith, for a time of Bible Study, fellowship, and the deepening of friendships!

Your children's ages may heavily influence your choice of a faith community as you consider what they offer in terms of Children's ministry and you consider your children's spiritual growth, not just fun and games. Be sure you know your priorities. Years ago, my wife and I began attending a smaller church in a store front that had the senior pastor's messages piped in via satellite. Neither of us had ever thought we would attend a church like that, but we found faithful friends, community, and, yes, several bikers in attendance!

If your life stage is one that allows more flexibility, the next section will be of great importance to you. For some of you, your children are very young and demanding, and you do not have much bandwidth to give and serve. Find a faith community where you can plug in and be served for a season. This is not a bad thing. This is the Body of Christ. If you are battling addictions, find a community that supports your sobriety — this is exercising wisdom. As a parent to young kids, you will be in desperate need of support.

FIND IT! Eventually, you can take your turn and BE IT (serve), but maybe not quite yet. That is okay. Give yourself some grace.

BUILD COMMUNITY
(BE)

Being community is the other side of this equation. Serve families that have a special needs child. Follow your interests and see who else enjoys these same activities. You may find yourself building an incredible community where you are serving at your **Parent Teacher Association**, a church group, or a **MOPS (Mothers Of Preschoolers)** group at church. If music is a passion, be a part of a musical group of like-minded people — this is community. The intentionality you have here will shape how tomorrow goes. Life happens. Life can even fall apart.

Who is in your corner?

Are you in someone else's corner as their world crumbles?

My family does not do **Boy Scouts** primarily for the skills that can be learned there. We do it for fellowship and community, with the parents that have grown over the years to become our go-to community. Some have gone through crisis and we have been there to love them and serve them. When we have been in need, these families have stepped up to serve us. Yes, there is fun at the campouts and accomplishment as you complete a merit badge, but in the end, the best part is the community of friends.

Find a quilting group. Join the choir. Seek out things that will invite relationship, conversations, and vulnerability. It is amazing what is shared at night, in the dark, around a campfire. Most men do not open up well, but many will in this environment. I love that. Being a counselor, I love to talk deeply about life and will naturally seek this out everywhere, but for many others it is difficult to trust people enough to share.

Moms — you need community!

Especially when your children are young and demanding of your time, attention, and energy. When my wife was overwhelmed with two toddlers, she called our pastor's wife and asked if she could recommend anyone that might be willing to mentor her. She began meeting with a lady in the church weekly and then began attending **Community Bible Study (CBS)**[55]. CBS then became my wife's community when I struggled with my health. Having a community that she knew would pray for us and help in practical way decreased her stress. Galatians 6:2 reminds us to:

"Carry each other's burdens, and in this way, you will fulfill the law of Christ" (NIV).

Dads — you need community too!

Work isn't enough.

What you need probably isn't going to be what your wife needs. You are two different people. I have met regularly with a friend, or at times a couple of friends, over the years and I always look forward to the time when we can get together. Regradless of whether it is over lunch or taking a walk, we can pray together and be challenged by one another.

Couples — you are two individuals with unique personalities and needs. You are also a "couple" though and that "couple" can be thought of as a third person. Your marriage needs other couples in it, to have fun with you, encourage you, hold you accountable, and come alongside you in the difficult days.

Find, build, and be community.

Times of crisis will reveal how well you have done this.

What's Next?

Kevin and Sally have grown in their understanding of where they are as a couple, become more aware of themselves as individuals, and are more focused than ever on intentionally giving their children a biblical sexual ethic. What else do they need? They will need ongoing support. For some parents and situations, it will be difficult to share what is going on in their family due to the vulnerability required. I hope you can find a lot of your answers, encouragement, and community from those in your life. There are other options available to you though if those are unsafe, or if you need professional, experienced advice.

I have been in private practice as a Licensed Professional Counselor since 2000. A recurring theme I see in families, singles, and couples is that they wait to seek help because they are embarrassed and fearful to talk about that area of their life and they pull away from all community. I personally believe that most people's counseling needs could be handled among mature, fellow believers within the Body of Christ. We need to be the body and reach out and serve others with our gifts, friendliness, and a listening ear.

PROFESSIONAL SERVICES

We are fortunate to live in a day and age with so many resources available to help individuals and families that are struggling. For generations, people struggled silently and alone. Families kept mental illness, depression, addictions, and abuse under cover to protect themselves and those they loved. Though we still have a long way to go in removing the stigma of mental illness, it has entered the national conversation and I am hopeful that we will see even more changes in the years ahead. Please know that if you find yourself struggling, you do not have to walk this path alone. There are professionals across the world with training that can come alongside you and your family if you find yourself in need. As you look for a professional to meet with, you will need to consider both their professional training and if they will be supportive of your beliefs, values, and goals. If they are not a good fit, please don't give up your search for help. Call someone else. Keep calling until you find someone that is a fit for your family.

I am humbled every time I sit with a family and they trust me with difficult parts of their stories. I work with teenagers and children who are dealing with sexual issues. My favorite clients though are the parents of these kids as I help them determine where their children are at, captivate their heart, and lead them toward hope.

This book is just the beginning because we all know that a book won't do the work for us. We must get up, learn the skills, and implement new strategies. We are the biggest hurdle standing in our way. If you desire to dive deeper into these issues and be part of an online community that is learning, sharing, and growing together, I invite you to join me online at

http://wwww.HealingLives.com

Contact me at **www.healinglives.com** for professional counseling and coaching services as well.

Access more resources including video trainings and more content for free at **parentbook.healinglives.com**

I Can't Say That!

BIBLIOGRAPHY

Allender, Dr. Dan. *The Wounded Heart.* U.S.A.: The Allender Center, Audio training, 2012.

Allender, Dr. Dan. *The Wounded Heart: Hope for Adult Victims of Childhood Sexual Abuse.* U.S.A.: NavPress, 2018.

Amen, Dr. Daniel. *Healing ADD.* U.S.A.: Berkley, 2013.

Amen, Dr. Daniel. *The Brain in Love.* U.S.A.: Harmony, 2009.

Amen, Dr. Daniel. *Sex on the Brain.* U.S.A.: Harmony, 2007.

Amen, Dr. Daniel. *Unleash the Power of the Female Brain.* U.S.A.: Harmony, 2013.

American Board of Christian Sex Therapists. http://www.abcst.sexualwholeness.com

AWANA. https://www.awana.org

Barna, Dr. George. *Revolutionary Parenting.* U.S.A.: BarnaBooks, 2007.

Certified Family Trauma Professional. https://www.traumapro.net

Community Bible Study. https://www.communitybiblestudy.org/

DeMoss, Nancy Leigh. *Lies Women Believe.* U.S.A.: Moody, 2001.

Institute for Sexual Wholness. http://www.sexualwholeness.com

Kennedy, Gillian. "The Effect of Sexual Arousal on Risky Decision Making - Thesis." University of Lethbridge, 2010. https://www.uleth.ca/dspace/bitstream/handle/10133/3056/kennedy%2C%20gillian.pdf?sequence=1&isAllowed=y

Leaf, Dr. Carolyn. *Switch on Your Brain: The Key to Peak Happiness, Thinking, and Health.* U.S.A.: Baker Books, 2015.

Levine, Dr. Peter. *Trauma and Memory.* U.S.A.: North Atlantic Books, 2015.

Levine. Dr. Peter, & M. Kline. *Trauma-Proofing Your Kids.* U.S.A.: North Atlantic Books, 2008.

Lipton, Dr. Bruce. *The Biology of Belief: Unleashing the Power of Consciousness, Matter, and Miracles.* U.S.A.: Hay House, 2008.

Mullins, Rich. "Doubly Good to You." Song recorded by Amy Grant on album Straight Ahead. U.S.A.: Myrrh, 1984.

Pearcey, Dr. Nancy. *Love Thy Body.* U.S.A.: Baker Books, 2018.

Penner, Dr. Clifford. and Joyce Penner. *The Gift of Sex; A Guide to Sexual Fulfilment.* U.S.A.: Thomas Nelson, 2003.

Pope John Paul II. *Theology of the Body.* Lectures. Vatican City: 1979–1984.

Rainey, Dennis and Barbara. *Passport 2 Purity Getaway Kit.* FamilyLife, 2012.

Rosenau, Dr. Doug. *A Celebration of Sex: A Guide to Enjoying God's Gift of Sexual Intimacy.* U.S.A.: Thomas Nelson, 2002.

Rosenau, Dr. Doug, and Michael. Todd. Wilson. *Soul Virgins.* U.S.A.: Sexual Wholeness Resources, 2012.

Santinelli, J., MA. Ott, M. Lyon, J. Rogers, D. Summers, R. Schliefer. "Abstinence and abstinence-only education: a review of U.S. policies and programs." *PubMed.gov.* January 2006. https://www.ncbi.nlm.nih.gov/pubmed/16387256.

Sax, Dr. Leonard. *Boys Adrift.* U.S.A.: Basic Books, 2007.

Sax, Dr. Leonard. *Why Gender Matters* (2nd edition). U.S.A.: Harmony, 2017.

"Sexual Risk Behaviours: HIV, STD, and teen pregnancy prevention." *Center for Disease Control (cdc.gov)*. 2015. https://www.cdc.gov/healthyyouth/sexualbehaviors/

Sprinkle, Dr. Preston. https://www.prestonsprinkle.com

Tripp, Paul David. *Age of Opportunity: A Biblical Guide to Parenting Teens (2nd edition)*. U.S.A.: P & R Publishing, 2001.

West, Christopher. *Fill These Hearts: God, Sex, and the Universal Longing*. U.S.A.: Image Publishing, 2013.

West, Christopher. *Heaven's Song: Sexual Love as it was Meant to Be*. U.S.A.: Ascension Press, 2008.

West, Christopher. *Theology of the Body for Beginners: A Basic Introduction to Pope John Paul II's Sexual Revolution (revised edition)*. U.S.A.: Ascension Press, 2008.

Wilson, G. *Your Brain on Porn: Internet Pornography and the Emerging Science of Addiction*. U.S.A.: Commonwealth Publishing, 2015.

Yarhouse, Dr. Mark. https://sexualidentityinstitute.org

Yarhouse, Mark. and L. Bukett. *Homosexuality and the Christian: A Guide for Parents, Pastors, and Friends*. U.S.A.: Bethany House Publishers, 2010.

Yarhouse, Mark. and L. Bukett. *Sexual Identity: A Guide for Living in the Time Between the Times*. U.S.A.: Bethany House Publishers, 2003.

Zimbardo, Dr. Philip. *The Demise of Guys*. U.S.A.: Amazon, 2012.

"#EvolveTheDefinition" (advertisement), *Bonobos,* 2018. https://bonobos.com.

Endnotes

1 Institute for Sexual Wholeness. http://sexualwholeness.com
2 American Board of Christian Sex Therapists. http://abcst.sexualwholeness.com
3 Certified Family Trauma Professional, https://www.traumapro.net
4 Barna, George. *Revolutionary Parenting*. U.S.A.: BarnaBooks, 2007.
5 AWANA. https://www.awana.org
6 Leaf, Carolyn. Switch on Your Brain: The Key to Peak Happiness, Thinking, and Health. U.S.A.: Baker Books, 2015.
7 Ibid.
8 Pearcey, Nancy. Love Thy Body. U.S.A.: Baker Books, 2018.
9 Paul II, Pope John. Theology of the Body. Lectures. Vatican City: 1979–1984.
10 West, Christopher. Theology of the Body for Beginners: A Basic Introduction to Pope John Paul II's Sexual Revolution (revised edition). (U.S.A.: Ascension Press, 2008), pp.13-14.
11 Ibid.
12 Ibid.
13 "Sexual Risk Behaviours: HIV, STD, and teen pregnancy prevention." Center for Disease Control (cdc.gov). 2015. https://www.cdc.gov/healthyyouth/sexualbehaviors/
14 Santinelli, J., Ott, M. Lyon, J. Rogers, D. Summers, R. Schliefer. "Abstinence and abstinence-only education: a review of U.S. policies and programs." PubMed.gov. January 2006. https://www.ncbi.nlm.nih.gov/pubmed/16387256.
15 Amen, Daniel. *The Brain in Love*. U.S.A.: Harmony, 2009, pp.225-226.
16 Ibid..
17 Ibid..
18 Amen, Daniel. *Sex on the Brain*. U.S.A.: Harmony Publishing, 2007, p10.
19 Ibid..
20 Ibid..
21 Ibid..
22 Ibid..
23 Amen, Daniel. *Sex on the Brain*. U.S.A.: Harmony Publishing, 2007..
24 Kennedy, Gillian. "The Effect of Sexual Arousal on Risky Decision Making - Thesis." *University of Lethbridge*, 2010. https://www.uleth.ca/dspace/bitstream/handle/10133/3056/kennedy%2C%20gillian.pdf?sequence=1&isAllowed=y
25 Amen, Daniel. *Sex on the Brain*. U.S.A.: Harmony Publishing, 2007, p.53.
26 Amen, Daniel. *The Brain in Love*. U.S.A.: Harmony, 2009.
27 Ibid.
28 Institute for Sexual Wholeness. http://sexualwholeness.com
29 Allender, Dan. The Wounded Heart. U.S.A.: The Allender Center, 2012, Audio training.
30 Tripp, Paul David. Age of Opportunity: A Biblical Guide to Parenting Teens (2nd edition). U.S.A.: P & R Publishing, 2001.
31 "#Evolve the Definition" (advertisement), Bonobos, 2018, https://bonobos.com/
32 Sax, Leonard. Boys Adrift. U.S.A.: Basic Books, 2007.
33 Amen, Daniel. *Healing ADD*. U.S.A.: Berkley, 2013.

34   "#Evolve the Definition" (advertisement), Bonobos, 2018, https://bonobos.com/

35   Zimbardo, Philip. The Demise of Guys. U.S.A.: Amazon, 2012.

36   DeMoss, Nancy Leigh. Lies Women Believe. U.S.A.: Moody, 2001.

37   Amen, Daniel. Unleash the Power of the Female Brain. U.S.A.: Harmony, 2013.

38   Sax, Leonard. Why Gender Matters (2nd edition). U.S.A.: Harmony, 2017.

39   Ibid.

40   Rosenau, Doug. A Celebration of Sex: A Guide to Enjoying God's Gift of Sexual Intimacy. U.S.A.: Thomas Nelson, 2002.

41   Yarhouse, Mark. www.sexualidentityinstitute.org

42   Sprinkle, Preston. www.prestonsprinkle.com

43   Allender, Dan. The Wounded Heart. U.S.A.: The Allender Center, 2012, Audio training.

44   Barna, George. Revolutionary Parenting. U.S.A.: BarnaBooks, 2007.

45   Mullins, Rich. "Doubly Good to You." Song recorded by Amy Grant on album Straight Ahead. U.S.A.: Myrrh, 1984.

46   Rosenau, Doug, & M. T. Wilson. Soul Virgins. U.S.A.: Sexual Wholeness Resources, 2012.

47   Ibid.

48   Ibid.

49   Ibid.

50   Levine. Peter, & M. Kline. Trauma-Proofing Your Kids. U.S.A.: North Atlantic Books, 2008.

51   Ibid.

52   Levine, Peter. Trauma and Memory. U.S.A.: North Atlantic Books, 2015.

53   Wilson, G. Your Brain on Porn: Internet Pornography and the Emerging Science of Addiction. U.S.A.: Commonwealth Publishing, 2015.

54   Rainey, Dennis & Barbara. Passport 2 Purity Getaway Kit. FamilyLife, 2012.

55   Community Bible Study. https://www.communitybiblestudy.org

I Can't Say That!